The Day I Said Yes...

Books may be purchased by contacting the publisher and author at:

Cover Design: Humanitree House
Interior Design: Humanitree House
Publisher: ZION Promotions
Creative Consultant: Humanitree House

ISBN 13: 978-0692276495
ISBN-10: 0692276491
1. Spirituality 2. Self Help

First Edition
Printed in the U.S.A.

The Day I Said Yes...

A Novella by S. D. McCall

Acknowledgments

I want to first thank God for bringing me THROUGH this experience. Without my faith I don't know where and how I would have turned out. Secondly to my support team my sister who is my best friend, the one who knows me, my flaws, my secrets and my fears; My mom, what can you say about a mother's love? My girls, the exterminator and cupid, my kids, and all that prayed for me. Sometimes telling your story is just what the doctor ordered. I hope that my life's walk and our relationships are not in vain. We learn from each other and our experiences. Without any of you I would not be the person I am today.

Dedication

I would like to dedicate this book to the children in my family. To my daughter Tiera and my son Darryl, My nieces Shaunesi, Eboni, and Trinity, my great nephew Tacari "Man", I pray that each of you set and reach each goal in your lives and may God continue to keep you in perfect peace.

Love you all!!!

Lysanias (Hebrew word meaning: One who drives away sorrow; the end of sadness)

December 24, 2011

Status update: *"I do, I do, I do…. In my Young Jeezy voice" And I said YES!!!! (The caption that read under a nice shiny engagement ring that had been place on my finger)*

That day in front of the people that mean the most to me in life, he proposed. I was ecstatic, confused, scared and shocked all at the same time. The phones were whipped out and all the post began. My mom, my nieces, my sister, my kids!!! Oh my God was this really happening?

The post were seen so quickly over 175 "likes" and "comments" poured in:

"YAY!!! That's fantastic CONGRATULATIONS!!"

"WoooooooHoooooo so happy for you and your lucky guy"

"Congrats cousin….Congrats you deserve it!"

"You have struggled and kept your head above water, you deserve all the happiness…."

"I am so happy for you Keep God first and the rest will take care of itself. You go girl…love ya!"

"WOW that's fantastic CONGRATULATIONS"

"Awww when is the date????"

"I better be in that!!! JK I'm happy for you."

"Congrats…Happy for ya!"

"Wishing you the best, God knows you deserve it Congratulations Dee!"
"OH SH@! You do it then"

"So nice, glad to hear it"

"I pray for your total happiness"

"SO HAPPY FOR YOU MY FRIEND!!!!!!!!! TEARS OF JOY FOR YOU! I MUST MEET HIM"

Genesis (1986)

I grew up in a church with a large population of youth. Some of our ministries included youth groups, girl and boy scouts, youth choir and the junior usher board. We all got along well and we grew up with wonderful bonds and lasting friendships. Although I was friends with many of the girls at the church and developed lifelong friendships, Keesha and I became very close. I would go and spend the night at Keesha's home frequently and we would go to Skate Palace and Tryon Mall Theater together. We even dressed alike when we went out.

Keesha had a nephew named Danny that was raised like her brother, since they were so close in age. Danny would always bring his neighborhood friends to church with him; Tony was one of them. I was introduced to Tony through Keesha and Danny. Tony was dark-skinned, with the curliest hair I had ever seen. Danny had an older brother and sister and a younger brother. Sometimes his older brother would come to church with Danny, Kyle and some of the other guys they hung with.

We attended church pretty frequently and of course we, the girls of the church, always tried to hook up with the boys. Growing up in a church where everybody knew everybody, you knew who you would or dare not date because of their reputation. Many of the youth from our church took the chance anyway and got together and are still married today. I was a private person, so I often desired to date the ones that nobody else knew.

I was so drawn to him; he was quiet and had the prettiest smile. We played "boyfriend and girlfriend" for a while. I was introduced to his parents and we started "going out". Of course at the age of 12 and 13 we were definitely playing!!! There was no real commitment at that age however, there was something about that dark piece of chocolate with nice curly hair that kept my attention.

When I turned 15 years old I got my first "whip"; what we called cars back then. Keesha also got a car that year and you couldn't tell us nothing! Both of them were red and sporty. I had a Pony Ford Escort and she had a red Ford Hatchback. We cleaned those cars every chance we got! Tony was there each and every chance he could be. He would say that he could have cleaned my car so much better than I could.

"You don't put the spit on those tires!" He would say.

I responded with "Ok show me what you got!"

To my surprise he was so right! He hid the bottle so that I couldn't go purchase it myself.

"You will always have to rely on me for this shine" he would say.

I laughed and gave him that responsibility each time after that. Tony and I would talk on the phone and we would see each other when I would go over to Keesha's. Things were looking good for us. We only had a couple of weeks before school began. I was going to High School and was so excited! This meant that we would be at two different high schools trying to stay in this "relationship."

My high school was known as the rich school. My neighborhood was bused there; we were not rich! He actually came out of his mouth with;

"I know you are going to fall for one of those rich boys at your school."

"Oh so you think I date for money, I'm 15 years old with a job; I don't need a boy for money!" I said looking him dead in the eye.

"Oh that's right you are the privileged one that has both your parents in your house so you don't need anything from me or anybody!"

He would use this comment often when we would talk about anything. I use to feel sorry for him because he did not have both of his parents in the house. I guess he longed for that, but this has gotten old and I mean old FAST! In my younger years I could roll my neck and eyes well! This time shit happened so fast I got dizzy!

"Really now, am I supposed to be ashamed of that?"

"Diane, I am not going to argue with you about this; I'm just saying."

I stood my ground. "I asked you a question; do I suppose to feel bad about that?" *Crickets* "That's what I thought!"

"Ok Diane; I'm done with that conversation."

"Good; let's move on then."

Every time we had a disagreement he would try to push it under the rug and move to another subject. His excuse was that he saw too much arguing at home so he refused to argue with me. Every single time he ended it with a kiss, hug or silence; this time was no different. He grabbed me by the back of the head and kissed me deeply. Right there on Phillips Ave. all was forgotten; of course until next time.

Everything seemed to be normal; school started and things were great. There were times that I'd get finished with track practice and he would be there, waiting at the gate. I always wondered how he got from his school to mine so fast without a car. His school was at least a 15 minute drive away from mine and we got out at the same time.

Spring Track season was a clear indication that summer was on its way! One year of high school down and two more to go. Breathing hard and sweating all over the place I asked him,

"Hey babe, did you see that time? I ran the 100 meter in 11.1 seconds; my goal is 10."

"Yes but I think that you could have done better than that."

"Fuck that! What are you doing on this side of the world?"

Standing on the other side of the track fence with his shades on

and baseball cap pulled down low he replied,

"Watching you, needing you…"

Feeling the sweat roll down my back I laughed and said,
"Not with all of this sweat. I'm going to shower; wait here."

Feeling fresh, clean and ready to get something to eat, I walked out of the locker room looking for Tony. I spotted him on the bleachers sitting with his head down; hands together as if he was praying to the almighty for me to hurry up. I guess I would be too since it was a scorching 90 degrees.

"Hi there; I'm ready to blow this spot!"

"Good; I don't need a tan. Where to?"

"Godfather's Pizza!"

I know good and well if coach found out about that he would expect my time could have been better also.

Tony and I could talk for hours about anything. I felt so close and connected to him; this was going to be my husband. I guess the tingling I keep feeling down low is normal. I've heard my friends talk about their experiences but I have not done "it" yet so I had no idea. That day in that restaurant I decided to reserve my virginity from everyone else except the guy that was sitting in front of me. The summer was coming and that's when it would be. This guy right here loved me and he was and shall be my first love, always.

Me and my fast ass thought since I am a virgin and I LOVE him, I should share this with him so that no other fast tail girls would entice him at his school. Keesha decided that we would lose our virginity at the same time on the same day. All we knew was that we were not going to get pregnant! Keesha chickened out on me at the last minute. My personality was not about to let me punk out. She became the "watch out man" and I the warrior!

"Do Me Baby" by Prince was playing on the boom box and I thought I had lost my mind. I was lying there thinking, this is what your fast ass gets!
"Wait...ok now...no...wait...ok...ok. I'm ready...not too fast...ok ok ok ok ok...wait...do you have the condom on?"

These heifers lied; this shit hurts!!

"Diane, please calm down; I got this. I have the condom on and I will not hurt you. I am going to take my time and make this special for you."

Tony was the expert since this was not his first time. Low and behold I stuck with it until it was over, as any young woman would do. I thought, "Done it and don't have to do that shit ever again for life! Can't walk, can't sit, and can't stand for long, since my insides feel like they are falling out from between my legs at any given time."

I had to soak in Epson salt for two days, unbeknownst to my mom who thought the track field had worn me out.

I avoided physical contact at all cost after that. I continued my track obligations and engrossed myself in school activities. I blamed it on how busy my school schedule was. It worked for a while until I realized that he no longer came to the track to wait on me after practice and that he was not calling as often. In those days it was the pager and landlines. Cell bag phones had just emerged (which I didn't have). I also noticed that he would not return my pages anymore. In my mind that meant his feelings were hurt and he felt that I was not interested. I drove over to his house only to found out that his family no longer lived there.

Surprised, hurt and confused I asked Keesha what happened. She claimed she did not know nor did her brother. I found this to be very odd and different. After a couple of days on the couch crying my eyes out it was time to move on. My dad told me to get all the crying out; suck it up and know that it was his lost not mine. This was the first time I'd ever sensed the feeling of abandonment. It made me feel empty inside, but my broken heart was repairable.

Signed, Sealed and Delivered 2011

CIAA Tournament in full effect in the Carolinas! First time out since the divorce, kids at dad's house, tequila poured; I had my T-shirt and panties on in the mirror doing the hair! I am looking forward to getting out of the house and enjoying a night of adult entertainment. I have two of the world's best kids. A son named DeeJay, and a daughter named Dallas that I hope turns out nothing like me. Boy I was something else when I was a teen. They are well behaved and have taken the divorce really well.

My girls keep calling coordinating the evening's events, and making sure I had not changed my mind. My phone begins to vibrate on the bathroom vanity again. "I swear if this is Sasha again I am going to scream!" Oops….not Sasha.

"Why is Keesha calling me?" I thought. This is a surprise because I have not heard from Keesha in years. There was no anger or malice; it was just that life happened, and we grew up in two different lanes. I answered by speaker right before it went to voicemail. "Hello."

"Hi Diane, how are you?" I can tell we haven't talked in a while since most of my family and friends call me Dee now.

"I'm good...haven't heard from you in a while." Shit, shit, shit! I burned my ear!! Now the tingling starts….UGH

"What are you doing?" she asked.

"Getting ready to go out; why what's up?" I asked,
knowing good and well this is not a catch up on life conversation at 9pm on a Saturday night.

"Girl, guess who is sitting in my living room?" she asked.

Blank Stare How the hell could I guess that one?
"Not sure I can guess that one."

"Tony!" Keesha sounded like a contestant on the Price is Right!

"Tony who?"

"Girl don't act like you forgot your first love."

"Tony Williams?"

"Yes girl and he asked me to call you to see if it was okay to give him your number?"

Hold on, if remember correctly this dude became ghost about 25 years ago, and I had not heard or known if he was even alive. But now since he has RISEN I should be jumping up and down like I won the showcase.

"WOW... that's funny! How in the hell was I supposed to have guessed that? Well I tell you what. You can give it to him, but he need not call tonight because I am on the way out."

I hit the end button on the android and I laughed my ass off. Isn't that some shit. I checked the hair in the mirror, and outfit in the full length. #Ready

We pulled up to what was known as the hottest club in town. The line was ridiculously out the door, around the corner and down the parking lot.

"Get that look off your face girl."

My girl knew me well because I gave her a, "I'll be damned if I'm going to stand in that long ass line in these heels looking 'thirsty' tonight!" look!"I didn't even mention how cold it was. Charlotte weather can trick you in the month of March.

"Chic we are VIP tonight so watch your back as we walk past all these thirsty ones!"

Sasha knew how to plan and execute a great night out so I was not worried. Sure enough we even had valet parking. We pulled up, she handed the keys over and we walked right in. The music was on point, the crowd mature, and the drinks flowed. I danced until I could barely walk. Although I hadn't clubbed in a while I loved music and kept up with the latest dances, thanks to my wonderful kids. I had not been out since the divorce and it felt good. My ego was feeling on point. You see we were "newbies"; not those every weekend club chics that all the guys knew. We rolled up like we were some celebs visiting the QC for the night. Men were acting like men and ladies like ladies. This was surely a grown and sexy crowd that was not to be reckoned with. I enjoyed the night to the point that I didn't realize how long we were there.

My girls normally called me "old" since on a normal weekend I was in bed and sleep by 9pm. Not tonight; it was on and poppin' and life was moving in a good direction!

5 am Sunday morning is when I finally made it back to the house. I was feeling myself a little and it felt good. I made it upstairs, undressed and decided to sleep nude. Why? Because I could! As I closed my eyes I prayed, "Now I lay me down to sleep I pray the Lord my soul to keep…"

As soon as the sun peaked through my blinds, because I forgot to pull the block outs closed when I got in, I was awakened. The night was an awesome night. I was able to let my hair down with the girls and enjoy some great conversation, drinks and dancing! When I was young and called myself "being grown" there was one rule in my house. You are to go to church regardless of the time you enter the house from the club. I am lying here in this bed being held hostage, and being convicted at the same time. Up and at it I go. The journey from the bed to the bathroom on days like this seems to be miles.

Today is going to be a great day; breakfast, church and dinner. I showered, dressed; full and ready I headed down the steps to the garage to go praise my God. The day was bright and the sky blue. Days like this give me a natural high that adds extra steps to my walk.

My church has always been known for the music department. We had a range of music from the traditional hymn choir, to the youth praise team. We also had drums, guitar, bass guitar, bongos, tambourines, praise dancers, mimes, step team; even flag people (not quite sure what they were called) and the basic foot action. I loved to come to worship because it was always an experience. It jump starts my week and gives me a feeling of belonging, reassurance and power to persevere through all of the obstacles that life brings.

I walked in the house and opened all the blinds and curtains downstairs to let the sunshine in. I flipped on the tube to the cable jazz station and headed upstairs to change to cook. The kids would be home soon from their visit with their dad and my DeeJay can eat. I cooked the roast in the slow cooker while I was at church so all I had to do was the sides and Dallas' cornbread.

The soothing sounds of Bony James met me when I hit the bottom step. I love jazz; it really puts me in a calm soothing mood. My phone lit up, still on silent from church, and I looked down and didn't recognize the 910 area code. I let it go to voicemail but the person did not leave one. I was thinking "Who in the world was that...oh shit was that him?" I called Keesha.

"What is the area code Tony will be calling me from?"

"Hold on let me ask Kyle. He said it was 910. Why; did he call?"

"Yea but it went to voicemail and he didn't leave a message so I wasn't sure."

I waited to see if he would call again that day but he didn't. After the kids got home, we ate dinner talked about our weekend. We then got ready for the work and school week, so I didn't get a chance to return the call. I called Shay to tell her about the conversation Keesha and I had about Tony trying to contact me, and how he had called after church but didn't leave a message.

"You know he was quiet and shy back then. I hope he isn't still like that messing with your crazy tail" she said.

"Shut up girl, I'm not that bad. I will let you know if he calls again" I replied.

"Aight, talk to you later."

Driving home on Friday during the spring, when the sun is out and the temperature is 70 degrees or above is the best feeling. I get off at 4 pm so I have a good 4 hours of daylight left to do whatever. I hit my speaker on my phone to call the girls to see if they want to meet for drinks at the boardwalk. I decided to call Vicki first since she gets off at 4:30.

"Hey chica, do you want to hit the boardwalk today?"

"When?" she replied.

"Now. I'm off and can be there by 4:30 or 5."

"Ok I can get there by 5."

"Ok, see you then."

I then called Sasha and she said that she could meet us there by 5:30. Finally I called the kids cells to let them know where I would be. My kids were notorious for tracking me down if I do anything out of the norm.

I turned up the volume on the radio, opened my sunroof, and entered I-85 N. I love highway driving. I was driving like I was a race car driver in my previous life. I saw a state trooper up ahead; I looked down at my speedometer and slowed my ass down. Since I went back to my maiden name after the divorce my perks were GONE! I pulled in safely to the boardwalk, parked, checked the hair and makeup in the mirror before I got out. I had to make sure we got patio seating so we could people watch. Everybody finally arrived and we talked as most women do, about jobs, our kids, and relationships. This day was no different. I told them about Tony and how he had called last weekend but didn't leave a message. These two did not know him from back in the day but I had told them about him when we read a book that talked about your first loves and how it ended. I had been dating since my divorce but didn't feel like I was ready for a serious relationship, because sometimes the guys I would go out with would say or do something that reminded me of my ex-husband and it was a rap. Sasha would trip every time I would tell her about someone I met or went out with. She would pick at me and say how "green" I was at dating. She would tell me of some of the warning signs of men. I got married so young that I did not experience adult dating. Right now I am having fun and exploring adult dating. Although I prefer to be in a committed relationship, I want to make sure that I am ready for it.

Vicki thought that Tony calling was the cutest thing however, Sasha put on her suspicious hat. Vicki and I both laughed like shit and said at the same time,

"That's our girl!"

"Fuck y'all," Sasha said as she rolled her eyes.

"We love you Sasha" we all said in unison.

Well it was time to go. We laughed, had some appetizers and went our separate ways.

Saturday's Shine

Saturday morning in my house is cleaning time. I turned on the radio, woke the kids up and it was on and poppin'. Ammonia, Soft Scrub, and Ajax for the bathrooms was my thing since Dallas almost passed out one day she decided to close the door while cleaning their bathroom. Deejay was to empty all of the trash cans, vacuum, and sweep all the common areas of the house. I would have Dallas do the kitchen cleaning, her room and dusting; this was every Saturday! My kids also did their own laundry and had been since they were 10 years old. That was our Saturday morning ritual. I enjoyed it because that gave my kids a chance to talk to me, laugh, and listen to the radio version of their music. I can't take all the cursing. We were laughing and cutting up when my phone started ringing. I yelled to them to turn the music down or close my bedroom door since I was in the middle of wiping my bathroom mirror down.

"Hello, hello…." I said.

"Hey Dee, this is Tony" said the voice on the other end of the phone.

"Hey, how are you, I heard you were looking for me."

There is that chuckle I remember. "Yea I stopped by Kyle and Keesha's to say hi and I asked about you."

"I heard...so what have you been up to?"

This idle chitchat went on for hours. He told me that he had been married for 20 years but was divorced now with 2 daughters and how one of his daughters was in the military. He had been shipped to Wilmington to live with his grandmother, since he and his mom's husband had a fight. She told him to go there so he would not get into any trouble or do anything that he would regret. He said that he didn't have any grandchildren. He asked about Shay and my parents. I told him that my dad had died but my mom was good and she had remarried. I told him Shay had 3 girls. He vaguely remembered Antoine, my brother, since he was so young when he left. I asked about his brothers and he said that Ray would tell him things that would be going on in my life. He said that he knew when I got married, when I had the kids and everything, since he still spoke to Kyle on a regular basis. I asked if he was on any social media and he said that he was not. He asked if we could go out for dinner and a movie or something like that. I told him that we could and that I really needed to get back to cleaning. He said that he worked second shift so we would have to do it on the weekend. I didn't have a problem with that so we planned to talk again soon.

We talked every day before he went to work and when he had his "afternoon "breaks. He would sleep until 7 or 8 pm, get up and be on his way to work by 10:30 pm. Sounds like 3rd shift if you asked me. Anyway this went on for the next week or so. We finally made plans to meet for dinner. I told him where to meet me, which surprised him. He assumed that he was coming to pick me up from the house.

Two things were wrong with that picture:
1. I don't introduce everyone to my kids even though I knew him when I was young. We are grown now and I don't know the grown up Tony.
2. Safety is first and I don't think it's time for him to know where I live.

We met at Fridays' since the movie theater was in the same area. I wondered if he looked the same; maybe a little weight or grey hair. I made it a point to get there before our agreed 6pm time. He had told me what he would be driving (Red Expedition) so I knew what I was looking for. I backed in the spot where I could see the front door of the restaurant clearly. I was listening to Power 98 hip hop station, trying to calm my nerves. I saw him turn in, park, check himself in the mirror and spray on what looked like cologne. He had on jeans, Timberland boots and a tan leather jacket. To my surprise the once beautiful lock of hair was completely gone! I wondered if that was by choice or necessity. He weighed a buck-o-five soaking wet back in the day. Although he had some weight on him, it was well proportioned. Not bad at all!

I waited until he went in the restaurant before exiting my car. Before I could hit the alarm on my car my cell was ringing.

"Hey, I'm here; how much longer before you get here?"

"I'm walking in now."

When I reached the door he looked at me and did that smile thing that brought back so many memories.

"You look great. I believe if I would have seen you on the street I would have been able to easily pick you out! How is it that you still look the same?"

I laughed and said "Ok hun you are starting off on the right foot."

We had a nice "church" hug. After waiting a couple of minutes we were seated. The waitress came to take our drink orders right away. I guess she could tell this was the first date and we needed a nerve block. We talked more about where we had been, done and experienced in the years that we did not see or speak to one another. He asked me my definition of dating and I told him that I had friends that I would go out with. He looked at me like I was hiding something, so I cleared it up for him. I go out to eat, to the movies, talk on the phone; things like that. I don't sleep with multiple people if that's what you are asking. I am not in a relationship with anyone and I'm not planning on being in one anytime soon. He sat back as though he was trying to figure out if he believed me or not. I laughed and ordered another cocktail. He talked about what moves he wanted to make next and that he would love to have me be in his life permanently. He told me about his ex-wife; how she was giving him a hard time with the house. She was suing him claiming that he was hiding assets. He had been trying to sell his home in Wilmington for nearly a year with no luck. The realtor said that the economy was turning around, but it would be a long process.

He had 4 acres of land and he might be better off selling them in 4's. He talked about his oldest daughter being in the military and how he prayed for her safety daily. I told him that's Deejays plan after high school and that I can only imagine the worries. He talked about his other daughter living in Winston-Salem doing her thing as an attorney's assistant. I told him that he should be very proud of them both, then the conversation came back to me and my dating "thing." This is when I thought I might need to clear up some other things. "Tony you know I am not that same 17 year old girl you once knew? There are things that I want to do now that my kids are older. I have danced to others beat for most of my adult life and I don't plan on doing that again."

He seemed to have accepted that. After the movie he walked me to my car. He told me that he had a great time and would love to see me again.

"We will see" was all I could say about that comment. He hugged me, kissed me on my cheek and stood there until I pulled out of my parking spot to head home. Driving home, I began to think about could've, would've, should've….what would my life had been like? I believe I would still have 2 kids, and maybe not have lived in Charlotte. Would I have followed my dreams, would he have been a great provider, would he have loved me unconditionally, would I still be married? Can you really still be in love with your 1st love after being married and living apart with no contact for so long?

Did I feel anything when I saw him? It was great seeing him, talking to him and hanging out, but nothing major. Is this because of the life experiences that I've had causing me to live cautiously, and guarding my heart?

My 40th birthday was on the way and my friends and I were heading to Vegas! I'm so excited and absolutely ready to go. There will be six of us working our way through the streets of the city known as "sin city". The saying goes "What goes on in Vegas, stays in Vegas". Of course I told him about the trip to celebrate my birthday. He was somewhat reserved about it and said that he should put a ring on my finger to ward off men trying to talk to me.

I laughed and told him to stop tripping. The night before I left he insisted on seeing me for dinner. I would be in Vegas on my actual birthday day and he wanted to give me my birthday gift. We met at Friday's (I guess this was going to be our spot) for dinner. He handed me a card and a nice bouquet of flowers and I thanked him. We talked about my trip and how I should behave. I laughed "What do you mean by that?"

"You should act as though you are a taken woman" and he said that with a straight face.

I held my left hand up and waved it to him like Beyonce did in her "Put a Ring on it" video. He asked me to open the card and I did. I was not expecting any bills in it so when I opened it they fell on the table, in my lap and on the floor.

"Enjoy your vacation" He said winking.

"Thanks babe! If I win big I will split what I bring back with you" I replied.

We finished our dinner and headed to the cars. He gave me a kiss and a hug and I headed home to finish packing. Driving home I thought that it was nice of him to give me such a big gift. Hmmm...

What Happens in Vegas....

Vicki, Sasha and I arrived in Nevada first. We took the shuttle to the hotel, registered and headed to our room. We all pulled out our cells to text loved ones back home of our safe arrivals.

The Aria Hotel had been open for two years and it was extremely innovative with the automatic window covering, and side panel remote control for the lights and TV. The room had chocolate covered strawberries bedside my bed with Happy Birthday written on the plate. I was tired and jet lagged from the very long flight from North Carolina, but my girls were not having it!

"Get your ass up! You will not sleep in Vegas!"

"But we need to wait on the other girls to get here. We have a good two hours; I need a quick nap" I whined.

I headed to the shower so that I would be set on ready when it was time for us to dress and hit the streets. After I got out the shower and lotioned up I put the plush robe on and lay across the bed. I didn't remember closing my eyes but was awakened by Shay, Daisha and Lea jumping on the bed and yelling, "Happy Birthday!"

"Get up old lady!" is what they yelled.

That was when the party began.

Vegas was an awesome trip, we partied from the time we got there until we pulled up at the airport to leave. Our plan was to rent a car and drive to LA to visit Rodeo Drive. Although I was fooled by the weather; a wind storm in April, we made the best of it. During the day we walked the strip, and took snap shots with all the characters on the streets like Jason, Michael Jackson, and of course Elvis. The guys with the cards in their hands making a very weird clicking sound really got on my nerves. I finally stopped to ask what it was. It was a business type card advertising hooker services, and I told the guy no thank you! We had people inviting us to clubs, giving us wrist bands for free entry with drink tickets attached. We definitely took advantage of those. We had a little black dress night that I insisted the ladies participate in. We hit the first club that was way too young for us, and then caught a cab to the next one that was right down our alley. The decor was very lounge like with white couches spread about, and the balcony had a great view of the strip. This was the best shot for a girl's pic to remember this great night. I grabbed the waitress and she snapped a couple of pictures for us. Inside we were showered with drinks and dance invites. I sat back to take in the scenery and was very pleased. Shay was dancing with a very attractive, tall, dark and handsome type of guy. Sasha was lounging with her drink in her hand bobbing her head to the music. This hunk of a man interrupted my thoughts as he asked me to dance.

"Hello Birthday girl would you like to dance?" he said.

"Sure" and off I pranced to the floor.

After all was said and done, feet throbbing and all, it was a good day. The next day I had the opportunity to do the CSI experience. By the time it was time to leave I had about three full hours of sleep. That was...let's just say what happens in Vegas. We had a drink to toast for safe travels, hugged and we were on our way back to reality.

Stays in Vegas

Back in the Queen City I went back to my daily activities work, kids, school activities, dating etc. Tony and I still were talking and spending time together, however, I had not stopped dating others. I was out with a guy that I had been hanging out with for a little over 9 months and it was not the same. I didn't enjoy it like I used to. Every word was working my nerve and my mind kept going back to Tony. The date was finally over and I was about to head home. Of course, old dude knew something was wrong and asked. When I got home that night, I was lying across the bed trying to figure out my next move. I was used to being in a relationship for most of my adult life. I wanted that one person to share my thoughts, dreams, and aspirations with. Tony was coming over the next day and we were going to go see a movie. I was actually looking forward to spending some time with him.

I believe dating is like advertising to fill an open position. You know what the job expectations are and you know what type of characteristics you are looking for. You interview (date) perspective candidates and narrow it down to two finalist. You evaluate them both and then you choose the one best candidate for the job.
I heard a sermon once titled "This or That". The sermon came from the book of Joshua chapter 24, where the people were told to pick whom they will serve. When you make a choice, one of the two will be dismissed while making your final decision.

We went to the movies, had a great time and decided to grab something to eat on the way back to my place. I called the kids to see what they wanted, they said they had already gotten something and were not hungry, so we decided to stop at my favorite sushi spot.

When I arrived home, Dallas and Deejay were backing out of the drive way. "

"Where are you going?" I asked.

Dallas rolled the window down and said "We are going over to Nanny's house for a little bit."

"Ok, see you later." I replied as I pulled in the garage and hit the button to close it.

We sat down to eat and then the sleep; the ITIS kicked in. I took one end of the sofa and Tony the other. I know we slept for a good hour before I woke up. He had to go over to his mom's so I woke him up and walked him outside. As he was getting ready to get in his truck I said "Hey, I know you said that you wanted us to see where things can go, so I decided that I will not date anyone except you."

He stood there for a cool minute and then he smiled so bright, came over to me, hugged me and told me that I had just made him the happiest man in the world. My heart was very happy. I walked back in the house after he drove off. My phone lit up and it was him.

"I can't get this stupid grin off my face" he said.

I laughed and said that I was happy as well. I told him that we would see what comes of it. He told me that he never stopped loving me and I will not regret my decision.

Life was good and the kids began to warm up to him. I guess they figured if mom introduced him to us he probably will be around for a while. Tony was struggling to sell his house and land. He was paying a leasing agent to try and at least/rent it so that he would not have to pay the mortgage each month. The company that he worked for was going into their busy shipping season so he started working more Saturdays. Tony knew how much I hated pumping gas, so he would come over each Sunday to fill my car up and spend the day since at that point, was the only day he had off. God I love this man! Most days after work, I would stop by his place to maximize our time together, since he worked 3rd shift now. I picked up my phone and tapped his face and waited for him to pick up.

"Hello" he answered.

"Hey, what do you want to eat? I'm going to stop on my way over there."

"Is it 3:30pm already?" he asked.

"Yes, so stop slobbering and tell me what you want."

"Chick-fi-A will work" He said.

"Ok, I'll see you in a minute."

After backing my car beside his, I grabbed the bags out the car. I was not paying attention to the people that were in the parking lot to my left until I heard my name. I turned and saw a girl that I grew up with.
"Hey girl, how are you?" I asked.

"I'm good...do you need help?" she replied.

"No, I got it. How have you been? Do you live over here? How are your mom and sister doing? Lord my mom is going to trip that I saw you. "

"No, chile my son lives over here. Do you live over here?"

"No, my boyfriend does" I replied.

When I pointed to Tony's door I noticed her face changed; not quite sure what that look was for but it did. Now I have not seen this chick since I was about 10 or 11yrs old so I didn't think a whole lot about it. By the time I was about to ask Tony comes out the door to get the bags that I was carrying. He looked at her and I introduced them and told him that we grew up together. He looked, spoke and went back into the apartment. I told her to tell everyone I said hello. She did the same and asked for my number so we could catch up. No harm, no foul right? We exchanged numbers then I went in to have an early dinner with my man.

I tried to keep the excitement in our relationship as best I could with his sleep pattern and work schedule. I had been looking on the internet and reading some "keep the fire in your relationship" type books on a regular basis. I brought a lot of things to him, but there was one thing that I really wanted to try that one of my girls texted me. It was the helicopter! She sent this to a group of us that were in the book club. I looked at that text every day until I got up the nerve to try it. Well today would be the day. "I am going to send my babe to work with something on his mind" I thought. We ate and then it was on and popping. The French call it soixante-neuf (69). We chose the vertical version; him standing and holding me upside down. Everything was fine until it was time to release.....why in the hell did this fool dropped me and damn near break my neck! The pillow talk that day was not the same. I could tell that something was on his mind, then he went there.

"How do you know "the girl" in the parking lot?"

I told him "we grew up together. I met her when I would have to go to Earle Village in the summers, since my parents had to work during the day."

"I don't like the way she looked at me" he said.
I sat up on one arm so that I could see his face. "What do you mean how she looked at you? "

"I don't know...it was just weird. I don't get a good vibe from her" was his response.

I placed that response in my memory bank because this day was going to end on a good note!

Olivia

Olivia, the girl I ran into in Tony's apartment parking lot, called me and we talked for hours. Olivia and her sister lived there. She was catching me up on what had been going on with her and her family. She had 2 kids and was a grandmother. Her mom was still hilarious as ever. We laughed and talked until my jaws ached, then the questions started about Tony.

"How long have you been dating him? Where did you meet?" she asked.

Not thinking anything about it I answered them, beaming with pride. Every answer I gave there was an "Oh really? Good for you" type response from her. I'm thinking I knew her as a child not an adult, so maybe there was a little jealousy going on. Oh but I was not going to let that fly.

 "Do you know him?"

"No I just see him sometimes in the parking lot when I come to visit my son and grandson."

She changed the subject by asking if my sister still did hair. I told her yes and that I would tell Shay that she wanted her hair done. She said that she would send a friend request via social media so I could check out the pics of her grand kids. I told her that I would give Shay her cell number to get her hair done, and that I would check out the pics after I got the request. We talked a little while longer before I told her that I had to prepare for work. My babe called on queue as I hung the phone up from her. I told him that we had just hung up and he got really quiet. He said "be careful with her because I don't trust her."

"Ok dear...that's the second time you have told me this." I was starting a new job the next day as a Practice Manager in a Pediatric office. I was so nervous and excited at the same time. I was trying so hard to figure out what to wear. Tony told me to stop worrying because he knew I would choose the perfect outfit. I told him that I loved him and that I would talk to him when he called me on his break.

New Surroundings

My new position required me to manage two practices; one in Matthews NC and the other in Pineville NC. Although they are in two different cities, they were only 20 minutes apart and accessible by one road; HWY 51. I started my day at the Matthews office, was introduced to the staff, providers and where my office would be. I walked in, stood in the door way and the first thing that came to my mind was "I have a DOOR!" I tried to compose myself and act like it was no big deal. I immediately thought about Nia Long in the movie Best Man where she had on her head set walking around her office, being the boss. "Yep that will be me!" I thought as I was snapped out of my day dream by one of my Medical Directors who came in to introduce himself. Next I traveled to the Pineville office and the same process was done. I had a lot of training ahead of me so I was ready to hit the ground running.

The day was long but rewarding. I was able to leave a little early so I was going to make a beeline to Tony's to tell him how my day had gone. I walked out of the front door of my Pineville office and low and behold it was Olivia!

"Girl are you following me?" I asked and she laughed.

"No girl; I do the courier service for this practice."

"Oh ok, I just started today. I am the new Practice Manager here and at the Matthews location. I guess I will be seeing you often," I said to her as I was making my way to my car.

"I pick up and deliver there too." I turned and said "Ok, cool. If you need anything from me just let me know." I turned and continued that beeline.

Training was hard and tedious but a great challenge. I had gotten into a nice routine on managing the practices. I would run into Olivia frequently at the office more than Tony's Apartment complex. I was in my office of the Pineville location when there was a knock on my door.

"Yes; come in?"

"Hi...may I talk to you for a minute?" one of my nurse inquired.

 "Sure, what's going on? "

"We are having problems with the courier for labs. She is rude, disrespectful and never on time with the results or to pick up the specimens. Before you got here we were having the same problems. Can you please have a talk with her or her boss?"

"Absolutely. Can you give me some specific examples? Has she been here today?"

"No she has not been here yet. I sure can pull some examples. I have to re-stick a patient today because the lab said the specimen was not transported correctly."

"Please give me some examples before she comes to pick up today. Thank you for bringing this to my attention."

She got up to leave then turned back. "I know y'all are friends and I didn't want to say anything, but Dr. Smith was angry."

"Thank you for telling me; knowing her does not excuse this incident or any other in that case."

She left my office and I sat back in my chair contemplating how I was going to fix this. I picked up my desk phone and dialed the number on the card for the courier service. I spoke with Olivia's boss and let him know that I would speak to Olivia when she came into the office today. He was onboard with that decision. I thanked him for his time and told him that I would circle back around tomorrow to let him know how it went.

Olivia tapped on my door when she came to pick up.

"Hey, they said you needed to see me."

"Yes, come in and have a seat." I explained the situation that was brought to my attention and what action we had to take due to the error on the packing and delivery of a couple of specimens that she had picked up yesterday and a couple from earlier that week. I felt that she received it well until she was about to leave the office.

"Dee, to be honest those girls don't like me."

It took all of me not to roll my eyes. "Tell me a little bit about that."

She went on to say exactly what the nurses on my team said about her; that they were rude and disrespectful to her when she would come into the office.

"Please give me some situations where you have felt that."

"Well Tina, used to live in Earl Village so it goes way back. She didn't like me then and when she saw me here it started all over."

OMG are you freaking kidding me! Are we in high school? I sat there with my professional smile planted nice and neat. I took it all in and once this conversation subsided I reiterate what I needed from her as a courier. I didn't even entertain the latter. I did speak with my staff and asked that they keep personal feelings out of the office in the future.

Times are Changing

The weather was changing to fall, and it was time to set the clock back an hour. Most people get excited because you gain an hour of sleep. I did what I had to before the sun settled and temperatures dropped. I am not a fan of any degree under 60 so I would make it a point to be inside after dark. The holidays were on their way which was my favorite time of the year!

Everyone seemed so happy and I was already thinking of presents for him. One thing he liked to do was drag race. He would go travel about two hours; the halfway point from Charlotte, to meet his boys from Wilmington to drag race. One of the things that Charlotte was known for was racing and Memorial Day race was the Cocoa-Cola 600. I looked into getting tickets for that when I ran across "the race car experience" deal. I thought this would be the finale gift. I pulled out my credit card and purchased it on the spot. He would have the opportunity to suit up and drive the track by himself in a real race car. According to the ad he would have radio communication with an instructor at all times and his speed was what he wanted to do; no restrictions! PERFECT! My idea was to get him a gift for each month that we had been together. I loved gift giving by thinking of what that person has expressed they liked or by passive conversations during the year. Now that I have secured one I had five more to go and two months to get them. I decided on a titanium bracelet, some wife beaters, a couple of polo style shirts, boxers and a remote control red mustang. The story behind that mustang was, when he sells his house that will be the first purchase he was going to make. In the card I told him that although I couldn't purchase him the real deal he could play with this one. I wrapped and hid the gifts in my closet for Christmas. Now for the kids; all I could get out of them was "All I want is money." "SMH...I guess it's time out for me to try and purchase gifts for them now. Visa gifts cards it is!" At this point it was time to concentrate on Thanksgiving, which is my next favorite holiday. Tony and I discussed plans on how or where we would eat Thanksgiving dinner. He wanted me to go with him to his Mom's place since they ate early (2pm) and then we could go to my Mom's for dinner at 5pm. Sunday's was our day to be together since his work schedule was so demanding Monday through Saturday. Today he was going to church with me. A family that praises and worships together was important to me. I did not have that in my marriage and that's one thing that would be different this time. The last time that he was at my church when we were children; things had long since changed. We had two sanctuaries; one was designated for the youth of the church and the other was considered the main sanctuary. We also had a gym now attached and accessible through the main entrance. I could tell that he was thinking back on the yesteryears as he was taking it all in. Worship was awesome as usual. He got a chance to see some of the people that were a part of my youth era. Keesha was there with her family so that was a good surprise for him. We chatted with them a little after church, said our goodbyes and we headed to my house.

Drama

I received a phone call from one of my Pineville staff members. Usually when this happens they are trying to call in for Monday. She did not leave a message so I tried to call her back but it went to voicemail. I didn't know what to think of it so I texted her and told her to call me if she still needed me. As the night went on she did not call or text back so I thought maybe she dialed me by mistake. Another Monday rolled around and it was back to the grind. Pineville was my first stop for today. I came in and surveyed the facility and all was running normally, accounted for and working. I came out to do my rounds and Olivia was delivering the lab results for the practice. Things had gotten better since our last talk.

"Hey girl, how are you today?"

"I'm trying to stay warm; how are you?" I said as I looked over my shoulder to see what that noise was.

"I'm doing well. How's everything with the man?"

Ok now she has gotten my attention. "We are doing great. He keeps hinting around about what size my ring finger is. I keep asking him what he is getting me for Christmas and he won't say."

The first time her look changed back in the summer was when I saw her in Tony's parking lot. That look was an unknown one, but this one? No doubt in my mind that this chick knew something and was not telling me!

"What's that face for Olivia?"

"Umm, nothing really. Can I call you when you get off?"

"No, I will call YOU when I get off." With that I walked away pissed. I know it's cold outside but it just became like the Arctic in here! I am not playing with this girl, she better tell me something and stop putting all these innuendos in the air. The day could not end fast enough and as soon as I got in the car I pick up my phone to call Olivia, but Tony was calling me. I was not going to tell him anything about what was going on at this point I needed to get some facts together.

"Hey babe how was your day?" he said.

"Busy but productive. Why are you up already?"

"I want to meet for dinner before I go to work. Can you meet me at Chili's on HWY 51?"

"Sure I'll see you there." I pushed end call and starting dialing Olivia again. She didn't answer so I left a voicemail to call me back when she could. The entire time we were eating I was thinking. I do not want to start thinking anything negative about our relationship on innuendos that someone was throwing out that I had not had contact with for years. When things like this happen I always wonder what the motive is. Tony is not acting any different, he is working more (having to go in earlier) since his company has picked up a very large contract that needed to be filled by the Thanksgiving break. He was complaining his company was trying to add Sunday to their work week without taking a day away. I told him that I didn't think that was legal not to have any day off. None the less we finished dinner around 6:30pm which gave him about 30 minutes to get to work. I kissed him good night after he walked me to my car. I checked my phone to see if Olivia had called and she hadn't. See this is why I don't deal with a lot of females!

I really needed to talk to her; I had not told her that my position was changing. I had another position that I was offered and was starting in 2 weeks. I hadn't told my staff at either practice where I was going or that I was going in fact. If she didn't call me tonight I was going to call her tomorrow.

It was two weeks until Thanksgiving; the stores were already decorated with Christmas items. The mall was packed. Although I had finished my shopping I enjoyed the hustle and bustle of holiday shopping and being in the midst. People really seemed genuinely happy. Every year around this time Michael Jordan would release a shoe that my son just had to have. This year was no different. The difference this year is my daughter and niece also wanted them. My daughter had a part time position at a sports store and had gotten the sneaker fever. Before that job she didn't even own a pair of sneakers. She had to borrow some from her cousin to be in uniform. As you may guess DeeJay has been asking me nonstop if I was going to get them. The release day was going to be the Friday before Christmas. I told him "If I get these shoes they will be your Christmas present as well", thinking that would discourage him for getting them. Didn't happen; he still wanted them!

Thanksgiving morning I got up, put on the radio to listen to the holiday music. I was getting ready to cook breakfast for the kids and myself. We would be going in different directions; they would go to their dad's side of the family then meet me at my mom's house. I was going with Tony to his mom's to eat and then meet my family at my mom's. I cleaned the kitchen from breakfast, packed the car with the dishes I was to take to my mom's house and went up to get ready to leave. For some reason I was a little nervous. I hadn't seen his mom or family, except Ray, since we started back talking. If he was on the phone with them they would tell him to tell me hello and vice versa, but I had not seen them.

Tony came to get me from the house. Because of my nerves I forgot he was driving, so we had to unpack my car and put the things in his. He was seriously laughing at me.

"This is not funny!" I said.

"Yes it is sweetie. Why are you so nervous; you know my mom."
"I don't know...maybe because it has been so long. I have a funny feeling that this is not going to go well."

"Relax, it will be fine."

We finally got to his mother's house. I just sat in the car when he came around and opened the door. I just couldn't shake the feeling in the pit of my stomach.

"Are you going to get out?"
"Yea, just give me a minute."

"Are you sick?"

"No, it's nothing, I'm good. Let's go."

We arrived before the rest of his siblings and family. I walked in behind him; his mother looked at me and smiled. She said that I looked exactly same. She hugged me and told me to pull up a chair so we could talk while she finished getting dinner ready. I did, and she began asking about my family and what I had been up to. I of course filled her in, and she was nodding her head in acknowledgement. She would ask for clarity at times (when I am nervous I speak fast) but overall the conversation went well.

Tony's nephew and family came in next. I was introduced to them as Dee. I could understand that he didn't have to introduce me to his mom because we knew each other so I was taken aback a little with that. His oldest brother Ray came out next; again no introduction necessary. His youngest brother did not live in Charlotte anymore and we knew he was not going to be there. Here is where things got a little weird. His sister who was the oldest of them all came in.

First, she was wearing a God awful wig that looked like road kill. Next she had on a leopard print pair of leggings, high heel red stilettos and a red sweater.

As soon as she came into the room she began to scope out the guest. Her eyes landed on me and there is where they stayed.

"Who are you?" Before I could answer Tony stepped in "Cindy, you don't remember Diane but they called her Dee? "

"No; where would I remember her from?"

"We dated when we lived on Phillips Ave."

"She does look familiar."

"She was Keesha's best friend with the red Escort?"

She was trying very hard by this time to jog her own memory.

"Oh yeah I remember now."

She turns to me and said "good to see you."

We sat down, blessed the food and made our plates. We sat around the table like they did on the movie Soul Food. All the food was in the middle of the table so we had to pass each dish to one another. I put things on my plate that I had eaten before so that I would not be rude if I ate something new and didn't like it. By the time we were done passing, I had turkey, dressing, potato salad, green beans, and a dinner roll. Sugar hill Gang said it best in the lyrics to "Rappers Delight"; the food was horrible! The turkey with gravy, was dry as shit, the potato salad taste like a heap of celery and the green beans were sweet like southern ice tea!

I was done. All I ate was the dinner roll. Of course his mom noticed and I asked was a full? I told her that I was trying to save room so I could eat at my mom's and she told me to wrap it up for later. That's exactly what I did, with a smile.

Throughout dinner I would catch Cindy watching me, and then she would look away. I wasn't sure if she had caught my facial expression when I put the first fork full of food in my mouth or what. All I know is I was not going to eat that damn food. We played this little cat and mouse game for the remainder of my visit so I believed that it was more than that.

When Tony and I got in the car I mentioned to him what had taken place and he said that his sister is very protective over her brothers and it was nothing.

"She knows how bad my marriage was so she is cautious of who I date."

"But you didn't introduce me to her as your girlfriend."

He looked at me as though I said something crazy.

"She knows you are my girlfriend."

Whatever that was I was not going to let it ruin my time with my family so I let it go. We arrived at my mom's house shortly after that. We unloaded the car and headed to the house. I waived at my mom's neighbor who is also my mechanic. By the time we reached the porch my niece had opened the door to let us in. My mom had not seen Tony since the last time we dated but I told her that we had re-connected, I was seeing him again and that it was getting serious. Everybody was in the house laughing, singing, drinking and having a wonderful time. This is how we do every time we got together. I always enjoy the time I spend with my family. We are small and close. My mom had gotten remarried three years prior, his family was larger than ours so they would come to the holiday gatherings as well.

My brother tries to act like the daddy of Shay and I most days, and this was not going to be any different. He checked Tony out when he came through the door like "Who is this dude?" I introduced them and Tony said that he vaguely remembered him, since there was a 12 year gap between my brother and me, making my brother much younger than us then. The family treated Tony like he had been around for years. He felt relaxed and comfortable in their presence. We brought out the cards after dinner to play some spades. We turned up the music and had a wonderful time. Tony was laughing and talking with my brother and mom's husband. They were watching football in the den and talking junk to each other. We had to pull names before everyone scattered. I told Tony that my family pulls names on Thanksgiving and exchange gifts Christmas Eve, since both my sister and I had kids that went to their father's side of the family on Christmas Day. He was all in and pulled names with us. My brother was going to host this year and that meant he had to cook dinner too.

"We all better be full when we get there!" I teased him.

He threw a bedroom shoe at me. We were all cracking up!

Thanksgiving was over so Tony and I headed to his place since the kids were going to hang out with their friends. Plus I had to meet my mom at Wal-Mart at 4am. If I was to go home and get in my bed she would have been short!

November in North Carolina was not necessarily one of the coldest months. Tonight the temperature was in the fifties; not bad for a November night. On the ride to his place I kept going back to the time we spent at his mom's house. I still felt that his sister either had something to say or didn't like me. I tried to go back and see when I first noticed it, trying to recall if I said or did anything for her to look at me crazy. This is not over; I will find out.

Black Friday I was at Wal-Mart at 4a.m. in the morning so I could get this flat screen. I'm thinking 4 am was pretty darn good for me until I pulled in the parking lot and it looked like I was the only one NOT in line! "Shit, I'm going home to get back in my bed" I thought. I don't do lines like this and this is ridiculous! I searched my bag for my cell to call my mom and see if she was in line, or did I need to get moving.

"Mom, are you in line?"

"No I'm almost there." If she could only see my face right now!!!

"I'm going home. I can't do this and it's cold!"

"Stop whining and get your ass in that line."

And then silence. Did she just hang up on me? I looked at my phone; yep she was gone. Needless to say I was in line by time she parked. After all of this nonsense I still didn't get the flat screen. Tired, frustrated and hungry, we left and went to the mall and I had better luck there. I got great deals on shoes and clothes for myself. The beauty of shopping early for everyone else is that I was there for me only. I finally made it home and I was so ready to jump in my bed to take a nap before Tony came over. I took a longer nap that I had planned. We were not going anywhere but I wanted to have been showered and dressed when he got there. We sat around that day watching old movies and a marathon of Criminal Minds; one of his favorite shows. He kept grabbing my hand and playing with my fingers. I was thinking this is new.

"Why do you keep doing that?"

"I was just seeing something." is all he said.

I shook my head and went back to watching the show. After a while DeeJay came down the stairs to get food.

"Hi Tony."

"What's up man, how's it going?"

"I'm good; just about to smash this right here!" He had a slice of pie on a paper plate heading back upstairs.
"Nope, eat that down here. You know I don't play that boy; always trying to eat up there beside that game. That thing is not going anywhere."

"But I'm playing with some people online"

I gave him the "look" and he wolfed down the pie, threw the plate away and took the stairs two at a time back up to his game.

I turned to Tony and asked him what he was getting me for Christmas? He told me none of my business. I laughed, "Whateva! You know I want that C series mister, white on white with blue tinted windows."

"Ok wait on it."

"I rolled my eyes."

Christmas was right around the corner. I had wrapped all of the items that I was going to. They were under the tree and I dared either of the kids to shake, unwrap, or lift any of them. I told them I know exactly how I placed them under there so I will know. The kids were going to the mall to try and get the new whatever number Jordan's he was going to release the week of Christmas. I reminded Deejay if he got those $200.00 shoes that would be his Christmas. They went on sale Christmas Eve night but he didn't care. He wanted those shoes so off to the mall they went to be in line all night. My text message alert went off in the middle of the night. "Deejay: YEA baby I got the kicks!!!" I text back "Good son, now go home." I usually don't stay at Tony's but I knew the kids would be going to their friends after the mall and I would be home to get the gifts to go to Antoine's that night to exchange.

I woke up feeling like a kid; Christmas Eve was finally here and I loved being surprised. I didn't have a clue as to who had my name. My family was good at choosing gifts for each other. I had a lot of stuff to do before I would be ready to go to my brothers' place. I told the kids that I was so serious about eating before going over there because if my mom didn't do the cooking I don't know what to expect. My brother is 12 years younger than me, no kids or wife and I had never eaten his food. Every time we had a gathering he would bring drinks. I kissed Tony goodbye, and told him what time to come to my place so we could ride together.

Most of my errands were on the way to the house. I had to hit up the ABC store, grocery store and pick up some household items from Dollar General, all on my path home. The kids were still asleep when I got there; I guess that all-nighter got to them. I didn't bother them to get up and help me with the bags like I usually do. I managed to get everything the first trip in the house. Most times I would pull in the garage and blow the horn or call ahead so they would be waiting to unload me. It's the Christmas Season so I'm going to be nice. When Tony got there we all were still getting ready. He was sitting on my sofa in my room very patiently. I told him that I was trying to hurry but he told me to take my time while he talked to the kids. I was going back in the bathroom and was like,

"What do you mean talk to the kids?"

He looked at me and said "Talk to the kids while we are waiting on you" as he was leaving my room. I thought that was odd but I guessed he was tired of seeing me change clothes. I finally made it down the stairs and the only light on was the light from the brown and red decorated Christmas tree in the corner. I changed the decorations every year but kept the same artificial pine with clear lights. They were all sitting there like lost puppies waiting on me.

"Sorry guys, I'm ready. Make sure you have your gifts for the names you pulled."

"We do" they said in unison.

"I need to get mine out the truck; I'll meet you outside."

"Ok Dallas lock the door; we are coming out the garage."

On the ride over to Antoine's, Tony was very quiet. We had to pick up Deejay's girlfriend before we hit the highway.
We pulled up to my brothers and there was a white C300 with a thirty day tag on it. I turned to Tony and was like

"Is that my car!"

He laughed like hell and said "No sweetheart; I wish it was." I just knew he had gotten it for me. Dallas, DeeJay and his little girlfriend were in tears when we walked in from laughing at me. Come to find out it was one of my brother friends' car. We did our usual hello hugs and greetings and the house smelled good. Antoine cooked chicken, macaroni and cheese, green beans and had some rolls.

"Awww baby bruh, look at you!" I had to tease him. "I hope it taste as good as it smells."

Dallas, Deejay and my nieces all were wearing their new Jordan's. Eb comes in singing "J's on my feet, so get like me!" They began to sing in unison, snapping pics with their cellphones; just cutting up. We were the last ones everyone was waiting on so we sat down to eat.

Antoine hollered "Spade time!"

"Nope; gift time" was my reply. Of course everyone agreed with me. We all went into the living room to exchange gifts. We started with my youngest niece, Tony pulled her name, she pulled Deejay's name, Deejay pulled Eb's name, Eb pulled Shay's name, Shay pulled Dallas's name, Dallas pulled Shaun's name, Shaun pulled Larry's name, Larry pulled Mom's name, Mom pulled Antoine's name, Antoine pulled my name, and I pulled Tony's name. So all the gifts were out and everyone was tearing open the wrap or digging in the gift bags at the same time. We all were showing our stuff off, laughing and having a good time. There were "Ooo this is what I wanted.....thank you .....I love it....yes yes yes" and all other gestures. Dallas said

"Tony don't you have something else?"

Everyone in the living room got quiet while I'm trying to figure out why. Apparently I missed something because everybody was looking at me. I turned to my right and Tony was looking at me like he had said something.

"What is it?" I asked.

He looked down at his hand so my eyes followed and there it was..... A princess cut diamond ring!

"Oh SHIT!" I looked at my mom "Sorry Mom."

He took my left hand and placed the ring on it and asked me those famous words. "Will you marry me?"

The room erupted into excitement, hand claps, yelling and for me tears. Tears of joy that is; I had no idea that he was going to ask me to marry him, let alone in front of all the people that mattered to me. My loud mouth sister yelled "What is the answer girl?!"

"YES of course!"

On our way back to my place the kids told me that he had asked them for my hand in marriage before we left the house. I turned to him and asked, "That's why you went downstairs to talk to them?"

"Yes I had to make sure they were good with it."

"And if they said no, then what?"
"I would have waited."

I looked in my rear view mirror..."Thanks guys."

When we got to the house I insisted that he open his tower of gifts. I told him why I chose each gift as he opened them. He was so excited when he opened the NASCAR gift I thought he was going to explode. That night was the first night he stayed over and the kids were there.

We lay in bed talking about the night and how it unfolded. "Thank you for reaching out to my kids before you asked me. You know how important family is to me."

"What did your girls say?"

"Rena said as long as I am happy she's happy. Janice is ok, she wants to meet you."

"I want to meet them too. I don't want to marry you until that happens. Rena will not be in the states for a while, But Janice lives only an hour away."

"Ok because when their mother got re-married she didn't give them that courtesy."

"Neither did my ex-husband; that's why I want to meet them."

"Well we will need to make it happen."

"Dee I don't want a long drawn out engagement."

"What time frame are you talking about?"

"Six to eight months." I shot straight up in the bed.

"Are you serious? I have some things to get done. Your house has been on the market for six months without an offer, you don't want to move here since I built this one with the kids' dad. Unless you are hiding money somewhere I don't think it would be possible to have three mortgages right now. I know that we are going to do something small but I was not the only person that got engaged during Christmas. I will try to get in touch with a realtor to list the house."

"That's all I'm asking. I don't need you to worry about the house part. I will provide that for us.

There will be no more of you paying mortgage once your name changes to Williams."

I gave him a quick kiss, and was about to go take a shower and start my day. "Oh, one more thing, I know you kind of looked at me funny when we first started dating when I said I was going to

Vegas for my birthday, and that I also had a trip planned to Dominican Republic in May.

I need to know that you will not have an issue with my ONCE a year girls trip?" He looked at me sideways.

"What if I did have a problem?"

"Thennnn, I will have to think of a way to convince you that you don't have a problem with it."

I began to kiss his neck, his lips, his forehead, his chest; his voice husky and low replied, "No I don't think I have a problem with it since you put it that way."

"Good" I said as I popped up out of the bed.
Laughing and still a little caught up he replied "Oh you are wrong."
I had a lot of things to get done. We agreed that since we both had big church weddings before that we would do something small and intimate. We both like water, so I had a couple of ideas floating around in my head. Since Christmas was on a Sunday, I was off today. I really didn't have any set plans but to take down the Christmas decorations, and clean up. There was a great deal to do since I went way out each year. Tony came outside to help with the mechanical deer and tree.

 "Why are you out here doing this by yourself? That is going to be my biggest project with you. You are so independent" he said as he popped me on my bottom and took the deer out of my hand.
We finished in record time which allowed time to get to the left overs we had brought home from my brothers' house. After I heated the plates up Tony said grace we ate.

"I've been kicking around some ideas on what and where we can have the ceremony. What do you think about Lake Norman? They have charter boats that you can rent to have events on that are not outrageously priced. I was thinking that we can have both the ceremony and reception on one of them."

"I like that idea. How much does it run?"

"I will call this week to check out the prices and let you know." I declare some food is just the best the next day. Spaghetti, mac n cheese, pizza and this BBQ chicken my brother had was so good; either that or I am just hungry. New Year Eve was on the way, Tony and I didn't have a whole lot planned. Sasha had invited us to her place to celebrate. He didn't have a problem with those plans so we had RSVP'd earlier in the week that we would be there.
It was cold as all get out that night so we were lounging in my room in the sitting area waiting on time. The events didn't start until 11pm. I don't even remembering closing my eyes, and the next thing I heard was the celebration. I looked at my TV and the ball had dropped in New York.

Tony was fast asleep on the other end of the lounger. I turned the TV off, and woke Tony to come to bed. I laughed to myself, "I must be getting old!"

Rock Solid 2012

New Year, New Beginnings! I was so happy to go back to work to show off my new diamond ring. My staff noticed it right away. I repeated how Tony proposed for what felt like a hundred times. I finally got back to my desk to start work. I was so distracted; I wanted to look up the Yacht's available for the summer months, look for a dress to wear and find a Realtor. I had to sign back into the system all morning, since it logs you out automatically after no activity for 10 minutes. I was not very productive this morning and now it was time for lunch. I text the other supervisors to see if they were ready for lunch. I was antagonized during lunch. All I wanted to talk about was the ceremony, the realtor and all that I had to do.

"LOL, y'all shut up! You know I like stuff to be in order. I don't like waiting to the last minute on nothing and plus Tony wants to get married in August."

"August, this year?" they said in unison.

"Now who's excited?" I laughed.

"WOW what's the rush?" Brandon said

"He says why wait? We're paying for it."

"I guess" was his reply.

When we got back to the office I called a friend of mine who is a Realtor to ask her to come by to list the house. I had no idea how long it would take and I know Tony said he would pay the new mortgage, but I didn't want to have to worry about my house.

"Girl I have so much to get done before August."

"I know you do. Don't set yourself up though, houses are moving;

I just don't know how fast I can move yours. I need to come by to look at it and have you sign the listing paperwork. What time are you available?"

"I can do any day after 4pm."

"What about tomorrow?"

"Cool, see you then."

Find a Realtor; check! Next I placed a call to Lake Norman Yacht Rentals. I made an appointment for Saturday to come up to check out all of the yachts available for August.

I called my girls to see if they would be available for Saturday to hang out with me.

"What are you trying to do?" Vicki asked.

"I have an appointment to see the Yachts at Lake Norman and maybe we could check out David's Bridal on the way back to Charlotte."

"Ok, I can do that with you."

"Thanks girl. Let me call Sasha to see if she can join us. Talk to you later."

Sasha was available too. Sounds like we are going to have a girls' day out! The rest of the week went by pretty slow, but I was able to list the house which was a big deal. Things had changed with the listing process since I listed my first house; more paperwork of course but it was done. Things were getting back to normal at work so I was able to focus more by Friday.

The Wedding Planner

My appointment with the yacht people was a little early but my ride or dies were right there with me! I just love these girls. Vicki is not a morning person but she sacrificed that shut eye for me. I told her just that!

"Girl shut up; you know I was going to be here."

We arrived at the pier to meet with Dianna and she told me about the different packages available for each yacht that was available in August.

"What can I bring on the yacht as far as decorations?"

"Anything, except candles with an open flame."

"What about alcohol?"

"You have to use our bar. You can have a cash bar or an open bar, but if you want to cut down on pricing, try to serve a signature drink and beer. If your guests want something different then they can purchase it."

"I never thought about a signature drink; that's an idea I like" I told her. Sasha and Vicki agreed. After we toured a couple of yachts I decided on "The Lady of The Lake." I liked the design of the boat and the feel of it when I walked in. I stood on the top deck looking out on the water and it was breathtaking. The sound of the water, the birds, the roar of the boats engine was exactly what I wanted my family and friends to be able to enjoy on our day. Tony told me to get the prices for him, call him when I had finalized the plans and got a final bill. He wanted to do the deposit today. I stepped away from Dianna and the ladies to make the call. I was so excited to let him know that I had found the perfect space but my call went to voicemail. I tried again and it went to voicemail a second time. Sometimes I had to call back to back to wake him up so I called again. This time he answered.

"Hey babe, I found the yacht! The total for food, drink, DJ and decorations with a 4 hour time is $5600.00. The deposit is $1500.00 and payment is due in full 30 days before our day."

"Ok, let me call and transfer some money so I can give you my card number."

"Ok call me back they are closing a noon today. It's, umm," I looked at my phone, 11:45".

"I'll call you back."

I placed my phone on the desk in Dianna's office as I sat down. I told her he was going to call me back with the number.

"Ok I am going to lock up so no one else will come in" she said as she left the office.

"What is he doing?" Sasha asked.

"He said he needs to do a transfer and that he will call me back."

"Oh" Sasha and Vicki said in unison.

Dianna came back to see if I had gotten the number. I looked at the clock on her wall it was five minutes after noon. I dial his number again. He answers in a huff. I got up and walked out the office since it sounded like a problem had occurred.

"Hey, I couldn't do the transfer" he said.

"Why?" I asked.

"I forgot I had a limit to be able to transfer since my ex-wife tried to steal money out of my account when I left. "

I felt Vicki walking up on me.

"Hey Dianna is ready to go. Do you want me to put it on my card and he can pay me back?" I turned my attention back to the phone.

"Hey, Vicki said she can put it on her card and you pay her back."

"What? Hell no! That's going to make me look like I can't take care of things."

"But Dianna said that was the only weekend in August available."

"I don't give a damn about that you're not going to make me look bad."

"Whatever Tony." *END* God I really miss the dial tone! Vicki and I both went back in to tell Dianna that I had to take a chance on the date still being available next week. She thanked us for coming and we were on our way.

"Do you still want to go to David's Bridal?"

If I didn't order a dress now it would not be back in time. "I will wait until next weekend because I'm not in the mood right now. Let's go get something to eat." My phone began to vibrate in my hand. I hit the ignore button. It vibrated again and I hit the ignore button. My notification indicating a voicemail appeared at the top of my phone. By the time we were seated and had ordered our drinks I decided to check the voicemail. Of course it was him trying to explain shit!!! He wanted me to know that he is capable of taking care of everything tied to the wedding and he did not need any help. He stated that I didn't understand the males mind on stuff like this, but I was not having it. I didn't call back; instead I held down my power button to turn my phone off.

Tony called me in rage later that day. I thought he was still upset about the deposit but when I called him back he said he had received court papers.

"Court papers for what?"

"My ex-wife is trying to sue me. She is saying that I hid assets from her during our marriage!"

"WOW! When is the date?"

"March 17 at 2pm and I got to take off for this shit since it's in Wilmington! This is some bullshit! I have not done anything wrong. She is the one I caught ass up in the motel.

I let him get it out. I can't even imagine going through something like that with my ex.

"Well if there is nothing to hide then go and prove it."

"I'm going to call my attorney."

"Ok let me know what he says."

"Why is all this shit happening now. Every time I get in a good place shit pop off. She is married; she needs to go on with her life. "

"Do you think she is tripping since she found out we are engaged?"

"I don't know but this is bullshit."

"Ok call me when you are done talking to your attorney. Will he answer on a Saturday?"

"If not he will call me back on Monday, because I am going to leave a message."

"Ok, talk to you later." *SMH* How can a female, who has already re-married, start so much stuff?

I know I would not be able to deal with any of this crap. He called me back and we talked more about the court thing.

"I want you to go with me to court."

"You know I will; I will ask off Monday when I get back to work."

"I want us to go in together. I can't do this without you by my side."

"This is not going to stop nothing we have planned. I just need to settle this."

"I know. I will be right there looking fly of course." I laughed about that thinking about us going in there with shades on, looking all professional and shit.

"Another thing we need to do is start looking for a house. I'm not going to see a hundred houses either Dee. Show me maybe two that you like and we will decide from there."

"How about three to choose from?"

"Fine then; three."

Court

As promised, I asked for March 17th off when I got back to work on Monday and it was granted.

I was all set to be right by his side. From what he had told me about his break up with his wife I don't see how she had a leg to stand on. He told me that he caught her in the act with a guy who use to race cars with him. She moved out when his youngest graduated from high school and went to the Army, so he had no reason to stay in Wilmington. His mom was here and Charlotte was still home. According to Tony the court date was moved, since his ex-wife needed more time to get the case together. They didn't give a new date yet; just said it would be continued.

"Well maybe this is a good sign that she doesn't have enough to take you to court."

"I don't know; she is sneaky so I don't know what she's up to right now."

"No need to worry until there is another date set. By the way I talked with a realtor named Lisa about looking for a new place. What is the price point you want me to look for?"

"Under $250,000, I was approved up to that amount, but that doesn't mean we have to spend it all."

"I know I know….Ok how many bedrooms?"

"I know we need at least 4 to 5 bedrooms and a 3 car garage, so the kids will have space and we also have a guest bedroom when my girls would visit."

"Ok I will let Lisa know what we are looking for Monday. What time are you coming over tomorrow or are you going to church with me?" "I'm going to church with you".

"Ok, I will call you in the morning. Luv ya."

"I love you too, goodnight."

We really had a good time in church and the spirit was high! We were going to pick up something to eat because he had to work tonight. I wanted to be able to spend as much time as possible before he had to go to sleep. He had brought a change of clothes with him to avoid going home before work. After we ate and arrived at my house he went up to my room and laid down until it was time for him to get up for work. Our sex life was being punished since he worked so many hours a day. My weekly gas fill was suffering also and I now had to pump my own gas. He still paid for it but I had to pump; that's the part I didn't like to do.

Monday I talked with Lisa and told her what we were looking for in a house. We decided to meet at 4pm. She was a hoot and had the strongest Boston accent! I signed the agreement to work with only her for the next three months, to try and secure a spot before we got married. It was February so we had time. Tony said that he would go ahead and move into the house until we got married and the search was on. Lisa and I met that following Saturday. She had sent me listings all week and I told her which ones I wanted to see, so we had a plan. We looked at seven properties the first time we went out, and out of those properties I liked two. I told her the agreement Tony and I had of him needing only to see my top three houses, and she said that was reasonable. It took three weeks for me to find the last of the three for Tony to see. At this point he was working seven days of week. He was getting frustrated with his job and was considering going back to his previous position. I would have to call numerous times after work before he would hear his phone. He started having a great deal of headaches as well. I keep telling myself that he would be back on his regular schedule soon; at least I am hoping.

"Hey babe" he uttered In his sleepy voice.

"Hey, how is that headache today?"

"Just as bad as it was yesterday. I talked to Tom today."

"Tom, your old boss…"

"Yes, He said that I can come back to Smithfield if I wanted."

"What do you mean you want to go back to Smithfield? Do they have a location in Charlotte?"

"No. I am so tired all the time. I called to talk to Tom and he said that I was more than welcomed to come back. I would come back in a manager's position instead of floor supervisor."

"How is that going to work with us? Deejay will graduate next school year. I prefer not to move him."

"I was thinking that I can go back and travel back and forth. I'd leave on Monday morning, stay there Monday and Tuesday nights, come back to Charlotte on Wednesday, leave on Thursday morning, stay Thursday night and be home Friday after work."

"You don't like traffic enough to do that. Every time I talk to you while you are driving you are cursing someone out or blowing your horn. I'm supposed to believe that you are going to drive four hours to work three times a week, I don't think so."

"I can do this Diane. I'm tired of working seven days without a break."

"Well we will see what Tom says when you talk to him again."
I noticed he used my government name not my nickname. He must be getting aggravated.

"I think I am going to take it. I will get my time with the company back with all of my benefits and pension."

"I understand all of that but I think you can make just as much here. I don't want to stop your desire to do this however; I need you to consider it carefully. What about trying to use your electrician license? I'm sure you can find work as a contractor."

"I don't want to do that, it carries too much liability insurance to work independently. I'm trying to purchase us a house with my savings."
I felt like this conversation was not going anywhere fast so I ended for now.

"I'm going to go ahead and start dinner...I'll call you back."

"Ok, please think about it some. I will not ask you and the kids to move, just to be patient as I drive back and forth. At least I will have the weekends off again and my hours will be 7-3pm unless we had training or a late meeting."

With that he said his goodbyes and I just hung up. Since I had pulled out the chicken from the freezer before I had gone to work all I had to do was clean and season it before popping it in the oven. I started the potatoes to have homemade mashed ones and cleaned the asparagus. My mind keeps trying to tell me that this is not going to work but I know how tired he is all the time. Our time now is limited; at least we would have some nights that we could be under the same roof. I need to run this by someone to make sure I'm not being selfish. I called Shay to see what she thought.

"Hey girl; what are you doing?"

"Driving home...what's up?"

I filled her in on what Tony was thinking about doing. She was pretty quiet the entire time until I told her how he was going to drive back and forth.

"You mean to tell me that he is going to drive four hours to work? Where is he going to stay when he is there?"

"Girl I wasn't even thinking about that. I didn't even ask. His boys are there so I would guess one of them. I must ask though."

"I would ask that and ask him how long does he really think he can do this? What about when there is bad weather? February March and April are tricky."

"I know I know…. I've got a lot to get out of him. I told him to try to use his electrician's license. He says it's expensive to carry the liability insurance. On another note I finally found three houses that he is going to look at this weekend."

"I'm glad you've done that. I know your realtor is happy she is almost done with you."

"Shut up! You make me sick" I said as I was cracking up. "Thank you for listening; I knew I needed to run this by a third party. The way I'm thinking about this, we would have the weekends together and a couple of nights during the week. I don't get that now and he lives and works in Charlotte. You know what I mean?"

"I do. I just know how bad he has road rage almost as bad as me!" We burst into laughter.

"I'm surprised you haven't used your horn at anyone since I've been talking to you."

"Chile I wasn't even paying that much attention. I'm home now though. Just get the full picture, you are going to marry this man so this is a decision that both of you will need to be able to deal with. I'm here if you need me. I need to get in here and find something to cook."

"Ok, I'll talk to you later."

The rest of the week went by in a blur. We were waiting on Tom to call back to see if he could get in the next orientation class. Tony said since he was going back to a manager's position there would be a training class that he would have to go to in Raleigh NC for a week. Tom was working on his salary and start date. In the meantime Tony said that he would continue working this crazy shift until he got the call. Saturday finally came and Dallas came with us to see the final three houses. Deejay was at a wrestling tournament that day. He would have to see the houses another time, or I would take him to the final choice on Sunday. Even though it was April, It was an extremely cloudy, misty and chilly day. Dallas and I would go and pick Tony up after I picked up his morning coffee. Lisa met us at the first house, then we showed the houses in the order of my least to my favorite. I felt it would work in my favor.

"This one does not have a three car garage" was the first thing that he noticed. Dallas said that she didn't even know these houses were back here.

"Hey Lisa!"

"Hi Diane, how are you on this cloudy day?"

"I'm great but these two may be a problem, "as I hugged Tony and grabbed Dallas' hand and walked to the first house. This house had a wonderful front yard with a long driveway and side entry garage. Although it did not have a three car garage, the driveway would suffice once we were married. There would be Tony's two cars and motorcycle, my car and Dallas' car. The house had a screened in back porch and a black rod iron fence. This was not my favorite floor plan but it had the five bedrooms and three baths. There was a small sitting area and dining room as you walked in and while the decorum was not my style at all, I could look past that. Dallas on the other hand, was not looking at the big picture. I kept saying she is only seventeen she didn't know any better.

"How do you like it?" Lisa asked Tony and Dallas.

Tony said "I think it feels small. I like the driveway and garage space even though it's not a three car."

Dallas didn't have an opinion on this one. We followed Lisa to the next house since she had mapped our day out. Tony reclined his seat to take a nap since he had not gone to sleep yet.

"Mom, I didn't really like that house. It's not like our house we have now; too many walls."

"Well I hope you like one of the other ones" I told her, smirking to myself. Yep it's working out just how I wanted it to.

We arrived at the next house within 15 minutes. I had to nudge Tony so that we could go in and see the house.

"We're here dear."

"I'm up; let's go see this one" he replied.

This house was a custom build with the 3 car side entry garage that we were looking for. The yard was not leveled in the front and had a two-story deck in the back. It had a huge pine tree in the front and I could tell that whoever designed that house put a lot of thought into the details. The entry was grand and there is a beautiful chandelier that has a nickel finish. I like that it featured a master bedroom suite on the first level. It was considered an open floor plan. The great room had a stone fire place that was wood burning. There were hardwood floors throughout and chair railing in the dining room. There are two set of stairs to this home; one went up to the loft over the garage, with its own full bath and walk in closet. Dallas quickly decided that's were her bedroom would be. Tony and I both laughed, since we had said the fifth room would be his man cave. The laundry room feels like another room. It was wired for a TV and has a folding table and red oak cabinets. All of the bedrooms are a nice size on the second floor. The one thing that I have fallen in love with is the deck. The house backed up to a nice lot with lots of trees and nature. I see myself out there in the morning sipping coffee and relaxing. That's where Lisa, Tony and Dallas found me when their tour was over.
"What'cha think?" I asked both of them.

Dallas was still stuck on the loft area being her domain; I laughed.

Tony said "The yard is not leveled and I don't think all of the vehicles will fit in the garage and driveway."

"I agree but I think the house itself will work. Let's go to the last one." We walked out and got back in the car as Lisa locked the property.

"You picked a good one" Tony said.

"Yeah, I don't think we need to go see anymore" Dallas piped in.

"Good one dear but we have one more to see. Sit back and take it down a notch."

The next house is my absolute favorite! I hope that Tony will think the same. He insists on financing the house so he's got to like it. From the time we entered into the development until we parked in front of the house the scenery is breathtaking! All the lawns are manicured (a service that's included with your homeowner's dues). Both Dallas and Tony get out of the car before I could say anything. The entry was amazing! To the right was an office with double glass doors. To the left is the formal living room that leads into the Butler's Pantry. From there you enter into the formal dining room. All of this area except the office and living room is hardwood flooring. This house has two staircases; one from the foyer and the other from the family room. The deck is the full length of the back of the house. The house is set on a crawl space so the deck is elevated, which gives storage underneath for the lawn equipment and things. There is not a sliding glass door to the back which I like. I felt like if the price point is over $200,000.00 there shouldn't be one. There is a beautiful gas fireplace, 5 bedrooms and 3 ½ baths. The kitchen opens to the family room so it's a nice, open floor plan. I could tell by the "oooh" and "awww" that both of them liked it. My plan worked perfectly and Tony began speaking to Lisa about the sale price and particulars. I decided to take Dallas back through to see which room she would want to be in and she was talking a mile a minute. The laundry closet was upstairs as well.

"Mom I don't have to tote my cloths up and down the stairs anymore. I can come up the second set of stairs that's so cool!"

"I was hoping you liked this one over the other two. What do you think Deejay is going to say?"

"He is going to go crazy! How big is this house anyway?"

"I think Lisa said 3000 sq. ft. which is about 1500 sq. ft. more than what we live in now."

"WOW!"

Dallas and I made it back down to where Lisa and Tony were talking. "I think we are going to write an offer."

"Really! That's awesome I knew you would like it." I wanted to jump up and down so bad. After Lisa locked the house, she and Tony decided to get together the next week to go to the bank to qualify for the house. He'd told me he had a pre-qualification letter at home. Lisa said that was great so it shouldn't be a problem.

"I'm so excited" Dallas said as we got in the car to leave.

"I am too honey" I said; I think I was glowing at this point. Tony was kind of quiet and said that he wanted to get back to the apartment. He needed to get some sleep before work the same night, so we dropped him off shortly after that.

"I'll call you to make sure you are up by six ok? I want to thank you for sacrificing your sleep to go see the houses. What day did you and Lisa decide to go to the bank?"

"No problem. You picked some good ones to see. We said Wednesday; she is going to send an email to me so I can fill out the paperwork before Wednesday's meeting."

"Oh ok. Talk to you later; go get some rest!"

Dallas talked all the way home about the house; how she was going to decorate it, what color she was going to do and how she was going to place the furniture. I could only smile and let her go at it because I was excited as well. I never thought I would be this happy again. I have a guy that is willing to BE the head of the house in action; not just words or default title. He is hard working and willing to sacrifice for me and my kids. I better get that dress ordered before I mess up our date by ordering late. Shay and I are going next Thursday to look at some, and I'm not looking for a traditional dress. I want something relaxed, fit but sexy. Shay's good with style so I know I will be fine.

Missing in Action

I have called Tony five times now trying to wake him for his appointment at the bank. Lisa has called, the bank has called but he still hasn't answered.

"I don't know what's going on Lisa. He must be really tired today. Usually it only takes a couple of times then he answers. I will try again and will call you if I can't get him." I tried once again to get him up with a phone call and text, but still no answer. I called Lisa to reschedule for 8 am on Friday morning so we don't run into this again.

"Thanks Lisa and I are so sorry he didn't make it today."

"Diane I understand that he works nights. I will see him on Friday."

"Thanks...bye."

I didn't try to call anymore; I just went back to work so that I can get off in time. I had already had planned to get off early to meet him. I finished in record time, said goodbye to my team and headed out the door. I am going to drive right to his place to see what happened. Before I got to his apartment my phone begins to flash, since I had not put my ringer back on.

"Hello."

"Hey...I didn't hear my phone...I must have been tired. I had to get up and use the bathroom and when I did I checked my phone and saw all the missed calls. I'm sorry Dee."

"You know I understand that you are tired. I didn't understand why you would make an appointment at three in the afternoon anyway. I rescheduled it for Friday at 8 am so you can do it before you go home."

"Friday I have a meeting after shift. I don't think I can make 8."

"What about 9:00 or 9:30 am?"

"I'm not sure." Ok now I'm thinking something is up he knows there are two other offers on the table for this house. I'm trying to be patient here. "I need you to tell her when you can make it."

"Are you getting mad? "

"Yes; I want the house and I think that it fits everything that we need and asked for. There are two other offers on it now so yes, I am getting mad that you are stalling out."

"I'm not stalling out! I was sleep. If the house is for us it will be there when I go. Why do I have to go to the bank Lisa said anyway I have a bank that I can use."

"I don't care where you go we just need to have an approval letter to present to the mortgage company. What's going on with you honestly?"

"I haven't told you but I received more court papers and now she wants half of my 401k and savings."

"How can you come back and ask for that if you are divorced? That's makes no sense to me at all."

"She thinks I hid assets when we were married so she hired an attorney to sue me for everything. She even wants the mustang."

"But you caught her red handed, ass up in some sleazy hotel."

"That has nothing to do with it."

"How the hell does it not?"

"Everybody didn't go through a cut and dry divorce like you. You walked away with nothing but the house and kids. You barely asked for child support. Some women try to take all, including my ex-wife."

"So you telling me that a woman, who is divorced and remarried, got caught committing adultery but can sue you for money she thinks you hid while married?"

"YOU DON'T BELIEVE ME?"

"Who the hell are you yelling at? I'm trying to make sure that I am hearing what you are saying. Don't take your frustration out on me mister. Shit nah."

"You right. I'm sorry I am frustrated."

"I'll talk to you later."

"Dee……"

CLICK Oh he gets on my nerves. How in the hell does this woman have so much power? I fail to understand this entire situation. I can't wrap my mind around this at all. I didn't even bother calling my sis since we are going dress shopping tomorrow. I let the conversation go and picked up Shay so we could head to David's Bridal. I filled her in on the nonsense I was fed yesterday. She was shocked and just as confused as I was. She really didn't tell me one way or another what to do, however it was good for me to say it out loud. I tried on so many dresses I was tired. The sales lady finally asked what type of ceremony was I having? I described the boat and how I wanted to be comfortable. She brought over a couple of bridesmaid dresses instead of what I had been looking at. I put on the first one that was more of a sun dress maxi style. It was cute and flowing but I didn't really feel it. The next one was a charcoal color T-Length dress that was strapless with a sash. I took that off quickly.

The last one was very different; peach in color, knee length, on shoulder, with a black accent belt designed by Vera Wang. I absolutely LOVE it! Shay paired it with a pair of black stilettos with a black satin ribbon ankle accent.

"PERFECT touch! Thanks SIS; that's why I brought you with me!"

"You are welcome girl...your phone is ringing."

"Who is it?"

"Tony of course."

"Answer it and talk to him until I get dressed." I hurried to dress since I knew he was on his first break.

"Hey, how are you?"

"I wanted to call and apologize again about our earlier conversation."

"I'm ok but I'm glad you apologized. Are you going in the morning to the bank?"

"Yes I told them I had to be at an appointment by 9:30 am."

"OK...thanks for doing this."

"Love you...have fun with your sister."

"Love you too...call me after the appointment."

I am waiting on the call from Tony, while trying to concentrate at work. I don't know why it's taking so long for him to call me since it's already pre -approved. This is not feeling right and I already decided that we needed to talk today. I'm not feeling the fact I still have not met his daughter. He keeps making excuses on why we can't take a trip to Winston-Salem, and I am truly against us getting married without it. My phone begins to vibrate on my desk. I looked at the face that smiled back at me.

"Hi babe, what's up? How did it go at the bank?"

"I didn't get to go. I got a call from Janice and I am on my way to Winston-Salem. She is in the hospital because her boyfriend beat her up this morning."

"What!!!! Is she ok? What happened?"

"She said that she was on her way to work. She got half way there and had to turn around since she had left her badge at home. She said that when she got back there was a car in her driveway. When she went in there was a girl there and they got into it. He punched her like a man Dee!!! I am going to kick his ass when I get there."

"Don't do anything you will regret. I know this has got to be hard on you." I wanted so bad to ask about the appointment but I couldn't bring it up now...Could I?

"Call me when you get there so I know that you made it safely."
"I'm pulling in now."

I looked at the clock on my desk and it's 10:05 am. That answers my questions. There is no way he would have been at the bank at 9:30, filled out the paperwork and made it to Winston in 45 minutes. Oh my GOD!!! Is this a sign?

"Call me when you get all the information. I hope that nothing major is broken or damaged."

"Love you…bye."

I hung up the phone and the hopes of getting the house. I placed a call to Lisa to see if Tony had called her. She answered on the second ring.

"Hi, Diane."

"Hi Lisa, I was calling to see if Tony called you to tell you that he was not going to make the appointment?"

"Yes, he said he had an emergency and would call to schedule another one when he got back to back in town."

"Ok, thank you Lisa."

"Is everything ok, Diane? It seems to me that Tony does not really understand that if we don't act on this that the other two offers may outbid yours."

"I know. I'm trying not to be pushy and make it seem that I am not sympathetic about his daughter. Can you check and see if the house is still available?"

"Sure I can. Let me call the other broker."

I placed my phone back on my desk to wait patiently on Lisa's return call. Things are not working out as I planned. I'm beginning to think I may have jumped the gun. Don't get me wrong, I love him and want nothing more but to be his wife. I just don't know why things are getting so difficult. First, the yacht, now the house; nothing that he was in charge of is working out. I think he may be getting cold feet about this whole thing. When he gets back from Winston we will talk. He called me that evening and told me that there were no broken bones but she had a black eye and bruising.

"We need to talk about some things. First, I love you and would like nothing but to spend the rest of my life with you. I am concerned with some of the things that have played out since our engagement. I have tried to plan for the ceremony, bought my dress and searched for a home for us. All that you have said that you were going to do has not been done.

He totally cut me off! "Don't go there Dee, my child was beat like a dude, I have my ex-wife trying to sue me and now I am trying to get a job that will not have me working every day!"

"First of all you WILL NOT yell at me. I have a right to tell you how I am feeling!"

"I have to take care of my business before we get married."

"Fine, I got that, you were the one who requested a short engagement NOT me! If you are having second thoughts then damn say it! Don't fucking divert your frustrations on me. I can tell you this; we will not be getting married in August since it is already the end of April. We don't have a place to have the ceremony, you are up in the air with this court thing, your house has not sold, and I have not met your daughter!"

"What are you saying Dee, are you calling off the wedding altogether or what?"

"I'm saying August will not be the date. I think settling your business is more important. From this point on I will not say or do anything with the wedding. I am not mad nor will I budge on this. This is what I need to ensure that our future will be on the right track." He didn't have anything to say. He held the phone like I needed to elaborate some more but I was done with the conversation. What he didn't know is I had set a hard date in my head. If things were not done or moving by December 31st this relationship was over.

Right after hanging up with Tony, Lisa called back and said the house that I wanted had been sold; another shot to the plans. UGH! We are at the end of April with no place to move, no wedding date and a whole lot of loose ends. May was fast approaching, with all of the things that I had going on I was ready to go to Dominican Republic for Memorial Day Weekend. The girls and I had planned this trip last year and it was paid in full. All I needed to do was begin gathering the items I would take with me. The weather was not so warm here so it was hard for me to get in the mood to pack. I needed a bathing suit too, and Tony wanted to go with me to pick one out. I was looking for a Tankini since I wasn't quite ready to show the world my stomach.
"Hey you want to meet me after work so I can look for a swim suit?"

"Sure, but I get to pick it out for you" he said.

"I'll ask you opinion; how about that?" By the time I had tried on four different ones Tony was so ready to go he said,

"Have you decided so we can go?" I laughed to myself; my plans always work. #projectbathingsuite done!

I also bought a couple of sun dresses and wedged heel sandals while I was there. I was really going ham in the mall. I bought a floppy hat, and another pair of sun glasses so I was pretty set for the Dominican. Tony was so ready to go that he suggested any and-everything to do to get out of that mall. I finally gave in and we left; not a bad trip at all. After all of that shopping, when I got home I pulled out the suitcase and began to un-tag my items, fold and place them in neatly. I simply can't stand a messy suitcase. I heard it's hot and sunny most days so I took a number of outfits. We received our itinerary earlier in April to tell us what items we may need so I went by that. There will be five of us on this trip since my sis wasn't going. I'm getting EXCITED; just a couple of weeks to wait to enjoy the white sands and clear blue skies of Dominican.

Countdown

"You have a wonderful day. I'm going to the office. I hope you sleep well." I was trying to balance my phone, purse and work bag as I got out of the car.

"Thanks babe. I love you."

"Love you too." I went into the office with a mindset that I was on a countdown to a wonderful vacation. I said my good mornings to the staff as I made my way to my desk. I had a guest waiting on me when I got there. Can I get settled first dang! I knew something was wrong once I got closer to Sanchez.

"Good morning. What's going on?"

"Hi Ms. Diane, I need to talk to you about something. Can we go to one of the conference rooms?"

"Sure, let me tell the team where I will be. You go ahead in there."

When I arrived in the conference room he had his head on the table. "Ok I'm all ears."

"I did something that I regret. I got caught last night cheating on my wife. I feel like I have lost my family over a piece of".... he looked up, quickly corrected it to, "a girl that meant nothing to me."

"The reason I am telling you this is I think my wife will come up here, since the person I cheated with works here." I sat there with my jaw on the table. What in the hell am I supposed to do with this?

"Listen Sanchez, we will not tolerate violence in this office. We have procedures in place if you feel like your life or anyone in this office life is in danger. I have to talk to Katrina about our next step. Do you feel that you can stay at work today?"

"I don't have anywhere to go at this point, so yes."

"OK, let me go and find Katrina so that the building can stay secure."

"I understand. Thanks for listening." He stood to walk out the door, and then he turned back to me. "I really feel bad about this whole thing. If only I could have the moment back to make a different decision."

Not to put salt on his wounds I said, "Don't we all wish that at times?"

Katrina was my boss and I try not to bother her with Human Resource issues. In the same breath I need to make her aware. After speaking with her, we made the appropriate calls to security and our HR representative to make sure we did everything on our end. I finally made it back to my desk to unpack my bag and begin work. All was well in the office until lunch. Sanchez went out to his car to grab a bite to eat and discovered three of his tires were flat. When he told me this I really had to suppress my laugh. If he didn't know, he will soon found out that insurance companies will not pay for three tires! I advised him to call a tow truck and have it towed to a tire shop. Another day; another dollar. I have a couple of projects that I needed to finish or have at a stopping point before I take off to Dominican. The next nine days of work were going to be tight. There were also end-of-the month items that needed to be done so I was on my grind. I changed my background on my computer to an island scene to keep me focused. By Friday I was exhausted but ready for the weekend.

Saturdays and Sundays were the only days I could see Tony for more than 2-4 hours. I am trying desperately hard to keep the fire lit. Tony calls me every morning on the way home, so I am talking to him as though I am still at my place on this Saturday morning.
Unbeknownst to him I am traveling right along with him. I have breakfast in the car. I plan to feed him in more than one way so that he will have a nice sleep. I got to his place first and backed into my usual spot.
"You're not home yet" I teased.

"I'm waiting to turn into the complex" he said.

"Oh ok."

"Why, you ready to hang up?"

"No I was just asking…"

"What do….is this you in my spot?"

I laughed and hit the end button on my phone. I needed to get the goodies out of my car. He was grinning getting out of the car, and shaking his head.

"Hey there babe, you are wonderful. Is that food for me?"

"Us."

"Alrighty then!" We went into his place; I to the kitchen and he to the shower. By the time he was done so was I. We sat down to eat then I served him dessert! He was in "Hog Heaven" *LOL*! I showered and by the time I dried off he was snoring. I gave his lips a peck and let myself out. Project night-night was a success! I didn't have a lot to do today; grocery shopping, cleaning and laundry and I was done by 2 pm. I decided I'm going to relax today. This week was a beast and next week would be also. I am going to flip through all of these channels and find me a marathon of something. Oh yeah; Law and Order marathon. I got comfy on the chase in my room. The next thing you know my phone is ringing and its three hours later. "Hello."

"I must have worn you out too" Tony said.

"Whatever! I came home did laundry and cleaned."

"Thank you for tucking me in today. You always think of stuff to do for me."

"You my boo" (in my ghetto, Sha'Nana voice)!

We laughed and talked for a little while longer until he had to get up and get ready for work.

"Call me when you get in the car."

"Ok, I'll get back at ya."

I love putting a smile on that man's face.

Dominican Sun

Dominican Republic here we come! Vicki and I rode together and arrived at Charlotte Douglas International Airport first. Sasha was on her way and we would meet Shonda in Florida, and her cousin in the Dominican. Sasha walked in with her floppy hat and sun dress ready for the island.

"Awww shit na! Look at you!"

"Oh I'm ready girl" Sasha said.

"Let's go have a drink since we are not leaving for another hour."

We arrived in Miami Florida for our two hour layover. Shonda came in shortly after we sat down at the bar.

"Hi ladies, my cousin's flight is here now."

"I thought she was meeting us in Dominican?"

"No, Dee she will be here in a minute."

"OK, here is the menu. Drink up!"

By the time Shonda's cousin arrived we had to start toward our terminal to board for Santiago Dominican Republic! Our final destination is Punta Cana, Dominican Republic. We decided to fly into the smaller airport in Santiago then catch a taxi to Punta Cana. We all climbed into a white minivan style taxi so he could take us on the one hour commute. I've been out of the country several times to remote locations; Ocho Rios Jamaica, Cozumel Mexico, so traveling on a non-American road was not scary to me. What did scare the hell out of me were the huge pot holes, no lanes and rude drivers. They would be within inches before one driver would decide to let the other pass. I decided instead of thinking my life was about to end each time, I would lie down on the seat, close my eyes and pray. We arrived without incident;

THANK YOU JESUS.

Punta Cana was breathtaking. In total awe, I retrieved my phone from my purse, texted Tony and the kids that I made it safely, then began taking candid shots of the water, the resort, and my girls. I even got in a few selfies. The Dominicans are beautiful people and the men are eye candy; Lawd have mercy! We decided to go visit the non-tourist area of Punta Cana. The resort didn't seem too excited about our decision. They provided a tour guide and transportation and driving into the city was so beautiful. The houses had a Spanish structure to them; Punta Cana is very hilly. There are Mopeds everywhere with complete families riding them. The male usually drives with kids in the middle, and mom in the back. I've never seen such a thing. The stores are equipped with the typical tourist items. I grabbed two of the nicest shot glasses for my collection. One had the Dominican flag and the other, which was a double shot glass, had Punta Cana on it. I will be testing these out tonight! Sasha, Shonda, Tina and Vicki all made their purchases fairly quickly so we were ready to continue our tour. We were going to see the "rich" side of town. The houses and store fronts there were a little larger than the others but not so different. The tour guide pointed out the graffiti to us and what it meant. The food was different in texture, but very good. Our driver stopped at the pier and we began to climb out of the taxi. I thought, "If I didn't have my family back in the states, I would stay here forever." The view was absolutely breathtaking. The water was almost Cobalt blue; it looked like a photo card. I couldn't believe how pretty this place was.

Life Goes On

Back in the states and reality life was moving forward. Tony was ecstatic when I got back. As soon as the airline gave the ok to turn on devices I powered my phone. Tony had left a text to call him ASAP! I hate getting those types of messages. The kids were to call him if something happened. I called him.

"Hey babe, what's up?"

"I got an offer on my house!" He yelled in the phone.

"Very good!"

"Did you like the offer? I know you didn't want to lose out on profit by putting the land with it."

"I think it's a fair offer."

"WOW that means I need to get on the ball with selling mine. It has taken you months to get one offer."

"I know right."

"I think I will put it on the market in June after Deejay gets out of school for the summer. Then I want have to worry about keeping the house tidy for showings. He has wrestling camp in July and Dallas has that 'bridge program' for college."

"Yes that sounds like a good idea."

"Let me get my bags together. I'll call you when I get to the house."

"Ok babe, talk to you later."

"Hey Vicki, Tony has an offer on his house! Girl I need to get a move on it. It took him a year to get an offer and I don't want to have two mortgages to worry about."

"That's good; I hope it goes through."

Time was winding down on the offer Tony received for his place. According to him the couple was having a hard time getting funding. Oh no; not another hurdle!

"Babe I'm sorry about that. How long do they have to get funding?"

"I don't know; they didn't say."

"Let's not jump to any conclusions. "

Summer Time

Deejay was excited the school was letting out in four days for the summer. He was happy for two main reasons. One is that he would be a senior the next year, and that he did not have to go to summer school for anything! It was time for me to put the house on the market even if Tony and I did not get one. My divorce decree stated that I would sell after Deejay graduated. Since the market was moving very slowly I should go ahead and list it to see how things go. I would call a Realtor near the end of June to list it. I had some minor touch ups to do so that it will show well.

I called a REMAX Realtor after the 4th of July holiday to come and list for me. She was a very well informed agent, and had the comps to show me what the market looked like in my area. I was not too impressed with the reality of the market but what could I do? The house went on the REMAX website the following Wednesday. I got a call that day for not one, but four showings that day. I had to set some parameters on the showings. I ask that they at least send a text one hour prior to showings so that I can make sure the house was available. This would help to control things and within three weeks I had a cash offer. I almost freaked out; I was not ready! I told Tony; clearly he was not moved by it. "Just chill and see what happens" he said. I went on to say, "In the offer the investor asked for the refrigerator, washer and dryer."
 "We will buy another washer and dryer. I think he asked for that since he was an investor."

"Alright, I hear you." Just like that he nipped that worry in the bud.

My agent called me the next day to let me know that the offer was not going to go through. The investor money was verified but he would not allow the bank to know who his LLC were.

My bank said thank you, but no thanks. I was back to the drawing board. For the next couple of months it was the same thing. I would get an offer then something would happen. The final offer in August was the one and things went as planned. The bank took the offer without any reservation. I was doing a short sale so I was not worried about that. I was told that it would be up to three months before I had to move.

I called Tony and said "Babe they accepted the offer! "

"They did? When will you close? I guess we need to start looking again for a house."

"They said not until the end of the year. I would like to stay on this side so Deejay will not have to change schools."

"I'm ok with that. I have to tell you that I have accepted the position back a Smithfield."

What the hell…"You did what?"

"Yes…I was about to call and tell you when you called me. I can't take this working every day. I will go to training the second week in September and the training is in Raleigh NC for a week."

I am sitting here not believing what the fuck he is saying. Aren't you supposed to make decisions like this together?

"So you have decided that you are going to do that crazy ass driving schedule?"

"I think it will be good for the relationship."

"You made a decision for the relationship without the other half of the relationships knowledge?"

"You knew I was thinking about it so don't get upset. You can do a short lease until we find a house or we can start looking again. You said you have until the end of the year to move and that's three months from now."

"Tony I don't think you get it. That was a major decision that you didn't talk with me about. I know you told me what you were thinking of doing but we did not discuss it."

"Dee I'm tired. I know this is the right decision. We can get married at the courthouse now and next year have a ceremony."

"No thank you; I will wait on that. Plus I still haven't met your daughters."

"It's your choice."

"I know it is. You know what let me call you back in a few minutes."
UGH UGH UGH!!!!!!!!!!!!!!

I needed my support team on this. I don't think I am thinking right about this whole situation. I try not to run to them for everything. My grandmother told me before I got married the first time, "Don't tell people all of your problems because when you forgive your man no one else will." This situation needed another set of eyes so I called Sasha; the one who will tell me what I need to hear and not what I want to hear. I filled her in really quickly and she listened very patiently until I got to the end. She asked me the same questions Shay had earlier, which I still did not have the answers to. Since I forgot to ask, she asked me was I happy with his work schedule now? If I was then I need to say something but if not let him get to a place where he would be happy.

"What if he told you to stay at that practice you didn't like? Make sure you are not being selfish."

"Thanks girl!" That's it; I need to support my man.

Sunday before Tony went to training we talked and laughed so much. He was completely relaxed and ready to start his new position. I'm glad I didn't fight him on this. I can see the stress drain right out of his face.

"I'm glad that you are doing this. I can see you are more relaxed."

"I am babe. I can't wait to get the training out of the way. My salary is right where I want it and Tom has given me all that I have asked for."

"That's what I'm talking about!!" I gave him a high five, but the love we made later that day was on a different level. If changing jobs did this; DAMN he should have done this 10 months ago.
I talked with him after class each night. He said that the company changed computer systems, and that's why he had to go to a week of training.
"Honey I have to go to Wilmington Friday to sign my paperwork so I can start October 1st."

"Ok, when will you be back in Charlotte?"

"Saturday, and we are going to spend the rest of the weekend together."

Smiling ear to ear I said "Ok, that will work. Good night babe." "Goodnight."

I hung up the phone and decided that I would take off a couple of days and ride up there to surprise him. Yep that's what I will do because he deserves a special night away from home. I plan to leave Wednesday after work, but my plans were not in line with the arrival of my great nephew. All is well; Tony didn't know I was coming any way. My little buddy decided to take his time making his entrance into this world. The nurses told me that he would not be born until Thursday so I decided to go home. Of course half way down Independence Blvd. he makes an appearance! Dallas was there and recorded it for me and my niece did a great job. I went home since I was going to travel four hours to see my fiancé, my man, and my boo. Tony called after class and we talked about the baby and how class was going. He said that he was tired and had to study and get something to eat. "I'll call you before I go to sleep."

"Ok, love you." I was getting excited to see him the next day. I was not use to not seeing him every day or at least every other day. I set my alarm for 9 am Thursday and planned to be on the road by noon. I wanted to get there very close to the time he got out of training with 45 minutes of wiggle room. I arrived in Raleigh at 4:30 pm so I drove to the mall to kill time. It was a beautiful September day; the sun was shining bright with 70 degrees reading on my cars dash. Yep this is going to be great; I brought alone some surprises too. I reached out to my brother in law (I guess you still call them that after divorcing their brother) to see what he was doing since he lived there but there was not an answer. I grabbed something to eat about 5pm. During the week when I talked to Tony he would tell me the restaurants that he was going to. He even said that he had walked over to the gas station to get snacks for the room. He didn't know that I was taking notes so that I could figure out which Holiday Inn Express he was staying. I asked Sasha to Google Holiday Inn Express with a Raleigh address and she said that there were only three. Tony had said that he had not moved his car since he'd been there, since the training was in the Hotel. I drove to all three but didn't see his car. I did see the Chinese Restaurant he said that he ate at and the gas station that he walked to but not his car. Sasha called me back to ask "What company was he training with?"

I told her "Smithfield Foods; why?"

"I've called all three hotels and none of them are having a training session nor have they all week."

My stomach started flipping.

"Say it ain't so!"

"Have you talked to him?"
I looked at my phone to see what time it was.

"Its 5:30 pm he should be calling me soon. This is usually the time he calls. I texted him and told him that I was here to see him and to call me when he got out of training. I am going to try him again."

Surprise

From what he had told me Thursday, when I went to Raleigh to surprise him was that he was going to have to go to Wilmington Friday and that we would spend all day together on Saturday. It is now 1 pm and I have not heard from him. I have texted and called him on both of his cell phones. I had a book club meeting on this day at 5 pm and he knew this so when were we suppose to spend time? My sister had come over to ride with me to the meeting; I just needed to know.

"Hey Shay, I will be back." I said as I was putting on my shoes.

"Where are you going?"

"I'll be back before the book club meeting starts."

One thing I can say is that I had never driven by my man's mom's house or where I thought he would be to snoop. Today the urge was overwhelming so I drove to his place first to see if he was there. I pulled in but his car was not there. He told me his truck was at his sister house since he had not renewed his tag and the apartments said they would tow it otherwise. I drove past Tony's mom house to see if he was there. Not only was his car there but his truck was as well! WTF (What the fuck) is going on?
I pulled into the parking lot and backed my car up so that it was facing the building, and I had a clear vision of his car and truck. I pulled out the cell and tapped his face; I picked the 704 number. It began to ring but went to voicemail. I ended that call and tapped his face again, and this time I chose the 910 number. It rung and then went to voicemail as well. I ended that call and sat there; now with tears in my eyes, trying to figure out my next move. I took a picture with my cell of his cars in front of his moms place, typed the word "REALLY!!!" and hit the send button so hard I damn near jammed my finger. I was so mad but I would never disrespect his mother, so I know I was not going to go in the building. I was shaking so bad as I called his phone again and told him that I placed the ring on the car

and to go to hell! I peeled out the parking lot to head back to my house. After I entered onto HWY 74 my cell started to ring. When I looked down it was him; I screamed "FUCK YOU" and turned my cell off. I was talking to myself; crying and driving. "This motherfucker think I am dumb…..do he really think I am 'that girl'…I don't chase no damn body……He must be on some shit..." As soon as I got home I went straight to the stash to pour me a stiff one. Cognac was my best friend right now. Shay came down stairs to see what was going on.

"Girl what is wrong with you?" I told her what had taken place and she just stood there with her mouth open.

"What is wrong with him?"

"I don't know but I am going to get to the bottom of this. "

"Vicki called and she wants to ride with us to book club," Shay said as I went to get some tissue to wipe my eyes.

"Tell her she needs to come get us because I'm about to smash this." I held up my glass to my lips and let the smoothness go down slowly. Shay and Vicki had idle talk while on our way to the restaurant that we were holding the book club meeting this month. My mind was a mile away. They were talking about the book that we had read and would discuss. One thing about having a great circle of friends is they know when you need to talk about something and when to let you be. During this ride they let me be.

We arrived a little while later. I checked my eyes in the sun visor mirror to make sure I didn't have raccoon eyes. All was good so we walked into the spot to discuss the book and fellowship with the group. That was a good distraction for a short period of time. At this point Tony's job had him working seven days a week so me going to his place after Vicki dropped me off would not be an option. I looked down at my watch as we walked out it was 7:15 pm. Tony was already at work so I didn't even bother trying to call him, but I did turn my cell back on.

It took my android a little while to power up. Once it finally came on I noticed that I had missed three calls from him, and…

One voicemail…"Oh so you are going to put me to voicemail?! I didn't see the ring and you need to stop tripping. It's not what you think. My mom needed me to do something for her. Why won't you answer the fucking phone? Whatever Diane!" *CLICK* I thought to myself, "Is he really trying to be mad at ME; using my government name?

After we left there we went to the boardwalk to sit out on the patio to enjoy the weather. It was still nice out; the sun was setting but it was still 70 degrees. Vicki, Shay and I sat on the patio and talked about what my next move would be. Vicki kept telling me not to jump   to conclusions. Shay kept saying fuck it! She was such a no non-sense type of person. I didn't say much, because I still had that feeling in the pit of my stomach that I could not get rid of. I knew that it wasn't good; I just didn't know how bad this was going to turn out. By the time I got home I was good and tired. Tony had not called at his usual break time and I couldn't sleep at all. I tossed and turned most of the night until maybe 3 or 4 am.

It's Sunday morning and I have awakened with the weirdest feeling in the pit of my stomach. The string of events are not sitting well with me at all. Thursday I drove all the way to Raleigh with the intent of surprising my fiancé. He has been training so hard all week, which takes three and a half hours, stayed there for two hours waiting on the so called training class to be over. I texted him when I got there to tell him to call me when he finished class because I was in Raleigh. I imagined his phone was on silent or vibrate since he was in training, so when I didn't get a return text immediately I didn't think anything of it. I went to the mall to do some window shopping and had lunch/early dinner as I awaited his call. 5 pm; no call and I waited. 5:30 no call; I call him but no answer. 6 o'clock I call and text; no response. At this point my temperature is rising and not for a pleasant reason. I am livid as hell so I put my home address in my GPS and headed back to Charlotte. Tears began to cloud my vision and I began to pray. I can say I know who to call on to avoid jail! I drove almost half the trip back before he returned my calls at 8:13 with that lame ass excuse.

"WHAT?" is all I could get out when I hit the green glow on my cell to answer.

"Babe, I didn't get your messages until just now. Where are you?"

"I'm on my way home and I am using my phone's GPS. I have to go."

"Wait! I'm sorry. We decided to go ahead and take the test so we could leave in the morning instead of Friday evening. I didn't know you were coming up here."

"It's called surprising your man; you weren't supposed to know I was coming! Goodbye Tony; I will call you when I get home since the GPS has taken me through these back roads instead of I-85."

Click. Lord I miss not being able to give people the dial tone!

When I finally pulled in my garage and headed upstairs at 11:30 and landed on the top of the stairway Deejay said,
"I thought you were gone for the weekend?" I kept walking to my room so that he would not see my eyes and said, "I changed my mind. Goodnight son." I texted Tony as I walked in my room, *home, goodnight* and powered my phone off. They say women are gifted with intuition from God and I truly believe it. I'm laying here contemplating what my next move will be. I know something is going on with Tony. "God I need you to reveal whatever it is that I need to know. I need you to make it clear on this day, Father. I ask that you be with me as I get up and travel over there to see just what it is that will be revealed. In your name I ask for grace and mercy to be able to receive WHATEVER it will be. Amen."

The house was quiet and it was not unusual for the kids to wake up on Sunday and I be gone to early service. So I felt there was no reason to wake them up to tell them where I was going today. I slipped on a T-Shirt and jogging pants and headed out. I proceeded down I-485 toward the Providence Rd exit. I needed to get there before I changed my mind. The speed limit on this stretch of highway was 65 MPH but I was pushing 80 all the while watching for the cops. By the time I pulled the Altima off the interstate my nerves were completely shot. The way to enter into his complex and where his apartment was, allowed a great way to see the front door before you pulled into the parking lot. When I looked down the hill, I found it strange that the front blinds in the living room and second bedroom were open. Most people who were raised in a black neighborhood never left the blinds open. The saying was "People can see what they want to come back and steal." By the time I turned into the parking lot and backed into my parking spot, I look up and see Ray; Tony's brother. He is walking to my car in pajama pants and a wife beater! I roll my window down and he says,

"Hey, ummm Tony told me to come and ask you not to come to the door because his wife and daughter were in there."

"His wife? You mean his ex-wife right?"

"What are you talking about; Tony is married!"

"What the fuck are you talking about Ray? Why would I be wearing this engagement ring if he was married?" I shoved my hand so far in his face he stepped back.

"Dee I didn't know you were engaged. Tony said that y'all were just hanging out while he was in Charlotte."

Now this dumbass thought I believed this. You are his brother!

"I tell you what, if Tony does not bring his ass out of that house in two point two seconds I am going in." The way Tony's apartment door was facing the parking lot and I had a birds-eye view on it.
There was not a back door so when it opens I will see it.

"Ok ok...damn Dee, wait. Pull over here."

"Why?" He looked over his left shoulder and guess who the fuck was coming from around the grounds keeper shed? Tony punk ass dressed in the same attire as his brother. He was looking all shook up and crazy; I wanted to drive over him! Now the people at this impromptu party were me, Tony and Ray. I think Ray stuck around to make sure I didn't kill his brother or maybe he was just being nosey. Either way he stayed. Tony would not come close to the car knowing how my temper was, and that I would fight a MAN. He stayed out of arms reach and, I told him that I was not going to hit nor run him over with my car. I began the conversation with the one question that I needed an answer to.

"Are you still married?" He stood there frozen. "I know your ass heard me!"

"Yes, but I was going to work it out before we got married."

"When exactly was that going to happen? I have sold my house, bought the dress, and flaunting this damn ring around like we had something." You know that I have to move in three weeks and you are supposed to be going back to Smithfield so you would not have to work on the weekends. I have allowed you to be involved in my kids life and I specifically told you that I don't do married men. Separation is MARRIED! So all those stories you told me about her suing you for hiding assets is actually about a divorce? You have nothing to say?"

Ray asked "You sold your house?" "Damn Tony what the hell are you doing?" I guess that's all Ray got out of my rant and rave.

I started to think about the situation that I was in. There is his wife, who is in the apartment, his grown daughter who is in the Army, and then there is me, Tony and Ray. I picked up my cell phone and texted my girls simultaneously, "We need to meet now at the lake. Be there in 15 minutes." *SEND*

"This shit is not over; trust and believe." I snatched my car in reverse barely missing his ass and drove off. Tears flowed and the speedometer rose.

Vicki called first, "Are you ok to drive? You can park and I will come get you." "No I will see you in a minute."

The next call was from Sasha, "What is going on?" "I will see you at the Boardwalk." I drove across Charlotte in 15 minutes and barely remembered stop lights, streets, turns, or anything for that matter. These two are my ride or dies and I knew that I could count on them to be there. I call them good and evil; not in a way that is degrading or mean. You see Vicki is the epitome of seeing the good in everybody and every situation, even if the writing is clearly on the wall with fluorescent colors. Sasha on the other hand, is suspicious of everything and all people. It sounds awful but usually Sasha hits it on the head every time. I have awakened my girls and pulled them out of their beds very early on this Sunday morning, yet they are here ready to be what I need most; a friend.

I was the last to arrive so I ended up sitting in the middle on the bench in front of Boardwalk Billy's. I sat there for about a minute not able to pull together my thoughts to tell them what had happened. I tried, but every time I opened my mouth to speak the tears beat my vocal cords. Finally Sasha started with the questions.

"Is it the kids?" I shook my head no.

"Is it your mom, sister, or brother?" I shook my head no.

Vicki is rubbing my back, I'm crying and Sasha is trying to get to it.

"Tony is still married." I felt both of their eyes on my face, yet I kept looking forward. Not because I was engrossed in such thought but from the embarrassment of the whole situation I had allowed myself to get into. I beat myself up for the entire ride over to the Boardwalk. Being vulnerable is the one thing that pushes me past the point of no return every time. Sasha must have asked me another question because the anticipation on both of their faces was apparent.

"I'm sorry what did you say?" Sasha repeated herself, "How do you know that he is still married?"

I told them what happened, what was said and that the wife and daughter were there.

"Did you talk to her?"

"No" I said.

"If you had the chance, would you?" Sasha inquired. I thought about that question and said "Yes."

"Let's go. I will drive because he doesn't know my car." Sasha looked at Vicki and we all stood up and headed to Sasha's new car. There was not a lot of conversation at this point. I think everyone was processing what had happened and what was about to happen. I can imagine Sasha was getting her words together to stand toe to toe with whomever we needed to. Vicki; I couldn't tell. There sure was nothing good that she could think of to get him out of this lie he put himself in. As before, I looked down the hill as we pulled in the apartment complex. This time the blinds were closed and I notice that his brother's car was gone. I guess he thought all was well and he could continue entertaining his WIFE and daughter.

I told my girls to stay in the car and if I needed them that I would come get them. Sasha didn't like that too well knowing that there were two grown women in there and Tony. I told her to trust me on this one, said a quick prayer to God to protect me from all hurt and danger, then exited the car. I know Tony well so I knew the minute I knocked on the door that he would look out the front blind to see who it was. I knocked and moved to the side so he would not see me through the peephole that I knew he would use. He opened the door; looked to the right and damn near shit in his pants! He quickly pulled the door up behind him; his eyes were so large. He had on the same gear as earlier, but this time the shirt was doing a dance right were his heart was. I've never seen a shirt move due to heart palpitations before in my life.

All he said was "Not now Diane. We can talk later."

I said "Oh so you're going to use my government name again?

No I want to talk now and I want to talk to your wife."

He turned away from me and rested his head in his hands as he leaned on the banister. This is when he saw my girls in the car.

"Why did you bring them over here?" he asked.

I told him "The way you talked about Joyce and her attitude, and how she showed out the last time you went to check on your house, what was I supposed to do? I told them to stay in the car anyway. Wait, what the hell does that have to do with you and all the lies you have feed me for the last year and a half?"

I see movement from my side vision and the door popped open. There she is, looking like a tramp in drag.

"Tony what's going on? Who is this?" I turned to him and said.

"Yes Tony who is this?" Tony does nothing but stand there shaking like shit. It was a dead silence since my girl immediately turned the music off and rolled the windows down to get a better listen. I guess Tony thought it was time to go back inside the house. Of course I followed right behind him and so did his wife. Since he decided to be mute I said "Joyce my name is Dee and Tony and I have been engaged since Christmas Eve."

She looked surprisingly at me and said "Joyce? My name is Deb."

At that very moment I think I lost consciousness without passing out. I got to the door and told Sasha and Vicki to come in right now! As soon as Sasha and Vicki crossed the threshold of hell I told them "this is not even Joyce; she said her name is Deb!" Vicki stepped up to question me like I may have not heard or told her the right thing. Deb tells Vicki that she and Tony got engaged Labor Day weekend and she thought something was up. She said she and her daughter were moving in today. The entire time this little conversation was happening I am scanning the room. I noticed that all of the pictures of me and Tony were now off the walls. I also noticed that he was still mute and acted as though he was watching an action movie on the big screen. The sound I made must have been something that no one in that room had ever heard before. I was so surprised that Sasha had not beaten someone down, cursed someone out or something. I looked at her and she was just standing there. The sound that came out of me was unknown to me; I didn't recognize my own voice. Tony is standing here and not defending me, telling me that she is lying, not begging me to believe him; NOTHING. He drinks coffee every morning and he likes it piping hot. I saw his cup on the bar beside him. Before I could get my hand around the cup, Sasha quickly ushered me out the door and into the car. I don't remember the ride back to the boardwalk and I had to convince the girls that I could drive to my house by myself. I needed that time alone. Vicki and I live in the same community so she followed me and I arrived safely.

"She said it feels like there's no air up here...like the Rocky Mountain High he took me to, has now left me void of the essential element needed to breathe. I've often wondered what beauty could have possibly adorned Lucifer that caused his influence to change the course of human history...until I learn of his story. Not only was he cursed, but like Satan after the fall, he spread his poison in my Garden of Eden; my Paradise. It's been said that an apple a day keeps the doctor away....but what about demons in human clothing?"-Lester B. Howard/Zion

Now came the hard part. Going into the house and telling my kids. Before I could get out the car my cell starts ringing. I looked down; I guess he got his voice back.

"What the fuck could you possibly have to say to me? I was there, I saw her ring, you said nothing, and you let me look like a complete ass! If I had to tell this story to my girls they'd have committed me immediately! I have to find a place to live, I have a fucking wedding dress in my closet, I have been house hunting with you and a REALTOR, I've sacrificed with your crazy work hours, you are still married, and you asked two different people to marry you and gave rings! Who does that? Why did you even come back into my life? I was minding my own business and YOU reached out to ME." I looked at the phone to see if he had hung up on me but I could hear music or the TV in the back ground so I know he was there.

"I love both of you" He said.

I laughed like I should've when someone crazy says something crazy. "Bitch you don't have a clue on the word. I tell you what; you love your new fiancé, wife and girls! Count this one out."
Mind you while I am sitting in the car listening to this nonsense Vicki is standing outside my car door listening as well. I am crying and screaming at the top of my lungs trying my best to wake myself up from this awful dream I must be having. She is telling me to hang up so that I can get myself together before I go into the house. I guess the kids heard the commotion outside because here they come down the drive way. I hung up on him, tried to wipe my face and put on my big girl pants to talk to them; Epic Fail! I lost it as soon as I opened my mouth to speak. We all walked in the house so my business would not be so exposed. I already felt like a failure; no need to air it to the world. I told my kids that I was not getting married and that he was still married so that would be illegal. They were more upset that I was hurting than what I was telling them. Dallas asked me for my phone and went outside. Deejay said that he was going to kill him and I said "No you are not son. You know I will be ok and you will not do anything that would end your life or take away your future over him. He is not worth it." Vicki was still there to make sure things were ok with me. My niece came down with my great nephew and asked what was going on. I told her and she was livid too. Of course she called her mom and told her what was going on; my family is small and very close. Dallas brought my phone back to me and I told all of them that I just needed some time alone. I went upstairs closed my room door, laid on the bed and cried.
My family allowed me the time that I asked for. I got up about 8:00 to

text my supervisor and let her know that I was not going to be able to come in tomorrow. Thank God for text because I didn't want to talk to anyone. Day two on the "sofa" was better than day one. I actually got up, took a shower and put clothes on before the kids got home from school. Deejay came to my room to check on me. He sat down beside me on my bed, looked me in the eye and said, "Mom you are the strongest person I know." Can you say water works! I told him that he was the "bestest" son ever! The funny thing is that he had no clue how much I needed to hear that. I made it into work the next day. I put on that armor of God, fake smile, held my head up and tried to pick up where I left off. I was sitting at my desk and my loan officer called about the house and how they needed to know my forwarding address. I sat back in my chair and closed my eyes. This cannot be happening. I just placed a call to take it off the market. I only decided to sell it as a short sale so that I wouldn't have two mortgages after I got married.

"About that; I have decided to take it off the market" I said. "That's not an option since you accepted the offer two weeks ago and the buyer is ready" She replied.

(Oh my God! I feel like I am about to have a stroke.)

"When are you looking to close?"

"In 3 weeks." "I have to call you back." I got up from my desk, grabbed my keys and went to my car to pray. I cried and cried and cried; "God I know I am a survivor because you made me this way. I need reassurance right now; I can't be homeless. I can't have my kids on the street...I need you right now. You said that if I ask I will receive. Today I am asking and today I need to receive....Amen."

I went back into my office, got on the phone and dialed one number to a set of apartments around the corner from my development. That would keep Deejay at the same school, since he was a senior, and one they had a unit available. I then dialed Duke Energy, made my deposit and told them that I would call them back that afternoon with an address and when I needed services. I called one of the guys I worked with and my brother, and told both of them that I needed them to help me move in three weeks. Roof over my head;

check. Lights; check. Movers; check. All other things will fall in place. I said a quick prayer of thanksgiving and continued to work. It's one thing to mess my life up but I'll be damned if my kids are going to be affected. Dee was back on her grind; I will always come out on top.

At this point I transitioned into survival mode. I had everything in place so I placed a call back to the buyer's agent to let her know that it was a go. I gave her Vicki's address because I had not signed a lease yet so I didn't technically have forwarding one. DONE! I had told the rental agent that I would be there after work with the deposit and first month's rent. 13611 Mount Pleasant Rod #108, yep that would be my new address. I looked at the agreement when I got back to my car with disbelief I was supposed to stay in my house until DeeJay graduated then put it on the market. At least that's what I and my ex-husband agreed on. This is one of the times that I wanted to kick myself in the ass for going all in. He was my fiancé right? Ugh!

The kids were excited to move to a place with a pool, clubhouse with an internet café, and pool table. It was a nice place if I had to say so myself. The pool area had a gas burning fireplace, gas and charcoal grills, and a tot lot. They had two dog parks as well.

I moved on a Sunday so I didn't have to worry about U-Haul saying they didn't have availability. The day of the move was bitter sweet. I had spent seven years in this house, painted every room, hung every picture, picked out the appliances, carpet, outside trim, even the lot that it was built on. The day we closed on this house was a day to remember. We had gone from a 1000 sq. ft. home to a 2400 sq. ft. home. I made sure the kids knew what kind of a blessing this was for us.

I wanted only the best for them. Their father and I were able to have them go to the high school we wanted and he was close enough to his company that he could bring the company car home as well. I drove clean across Charlotte daily but I didn't care because you can't trade in the night sky out here. I was close enough to the city without having to be in the city. I would sit out back, look up and see the clearest view of the stars. Our neighbors all moved in around the same time. I was going to be the first to break out and move. Bitter sweet......

I now remember why I didn't like moving. How in the hell did I collect so much in such a small period of time? After two yard sales I still had to make three trips to the apartment, and one to the dumpster. All of my stuff would not fit but I guess I should have known that since I moved back down to a 1045 sq. ft. apartment. I took off the day to unpack and get things in order. I had to do my kitchen and bathrooms the day prior, now I have to tackle everything else.

The kids were doing their own spaces. I was in the middle of unpacking my shoes when my cell began to ring. I didn't even look at the phone since I had my ear piece in.

"Hello."

"Hey Dee." I jumped up to look at the caller ID because I didn't recognize the voice; It was Olivia.

"Hi" I said, as dry as I could without flipping on her.

"I saw on your status that you and Tony broke up......"

I changed my relationship status back to single the day before, so I guess she had been stalking my page. Who does that?

"Yes, I am single again. What's up...I'm kind of busy unpacking some things."

"I had no idea how to tell you all that I knew about him. When I saw that you guys got in engaged Christmas Eve, I called my mom so she could tell me if I should tell you or not."

I sat down on my bed and braced myself to hear what she had to say. Although he had not called, come by or even tried to explain himself, I still wanted to know the whole truth. I had a feeling that I had not heard it all. She started by stating the obvious; I was not the only one he was seeing. The kicker was that not only did he have another fiancé but he also has a baby mama.

"What, wait did you say? He has a baby on the way? From this same person who said that he didn't want any kids since his two were grown and doing their own thing?"

"Yes, I'm surprised that you did not ever run into her. The last time I went to see my grandson I saw your car. By the time I came back out the door you had left and she was going to the door. "

"Are you serious Olivia? What does she drive?"

"A red convertible mustang."

I sat there for a minute because I remember that day clearly. I was pulling out and she was coming in, I remember saying that the car was on point. It was the prettiest shade of red and the top was white.

"Is she white, because who I saw was white?"

"Yes and she is big pregnant!"

"How do you know that it's his?"

"Because she was cursing him out, telling him that all she wanted from him was child support because she knows he is cheating on her. She said that come October he better be ready to split his check with her."

I absolutely had nothing to say. I was in tears again. This time they were not because I was sad but because I felt so damn dumb. I was so angry I could have killed him with my bare hands.

"Hello?" she said.

"I'm here. "

"I am so sorry for not telling you what I knew" she continued.

"To be honest with you, I probably would not have listened to you or believed you. This played out exactly how it was supposed to. I had not seen you in years nor I did I know you as an adult Olivia. Don't blame yourself because I sure as hell am not. The day I found out about Tony I asked God to make it plain, so I could not make an excuse for him or that I couldn't ignore it. I don't know what I'm going to do with this information right now. I am trying to get settled in my new place. I have a wedding dress to sell and I hope I can get something good off this ring."

"Ok girl, I just needed to tell you. I hope all works out for you."

"Thanks, again. I'll talk to you later."

Well I'll be damned! What else God! I dial Keesha's number and told her to have Ray call me ASAP. I needed to see what the hell was wrong with his brother. Since Tony felt like he had nothing to say, maybe noisy ass Ray could shed some light on why me?

It took him three hours to call me but he did.

"Hello."

"Hey Ray, what is going on with your brother?"

"Man, I don't know Dee. I told him that he needed to get his shit together. He has not been the same since he moved back up here. I was so shocked at the shit he had done once I heard y'all conversation that Sunday. He told me to lie and say that it was his wife in there. If I knew all that other shit I wouldn't have done that. We go way back Dee...I'm sorry."

"So your brother is still married, engaged to two people and has a baby on the way and you knew NOTHING about this?"

"WHAT baby?"

"Ray don't act like you don't know."

"I don't know about a baby."

"Well he does and she is due next month."

"Damn his grandkids and baby are going to grow up together."
I threw my damn TV remote across the room.

"What damn grandkids?"

"Dee you didn't know that he has two grandkids?"

"Hell no! By whom; Janice or Rena?"

"No by Trina."

"Who the fuck is Trina! Tony told me he has two kids; Janice
and Rena. Janice was a Legal Aid and Rena in the army, so
where in the hell did a Trina come from?"

"Dee...Tony has three kids and two grandkids."

I felt like all of the wind had escaped me. I am getting dizzy and I feel
like I am about to pass the hell out. There are no words in me right
now. I DID NOT KNOW THIS MAN!

"Dee? Diane...Dee...are you still there?"

"I got to go." I hit the end button on my cell, sat on the floor and
cried. What type of person does this to another human? I was
about to marry this...I let my guard down...I am usually smarter
than this... my kids...oh my God! I was about to have him in my kids
life! This pain in my heart is unfamiliar. I didn't feel this when my
dad died. I didn't feel this when I got divorced. This pain right here

is new and I don't like it one bit.

I didn't have the energy to call any of my support team that night; I just showered and cried. I had to get it together by the morning so that I could go to work. I jumped out the bed and pulled my laptop out. You can Google anyone so I powered up the computer and waited what seemed like forever. I went to Google and typed in his name. He didn't use social media sites so I was wondering if anything would come up. There were some with his name but not him. I even tried the sex offenders website; Thank God nothing came up. I did a reverse number search via the white pages next. I'll be a monkey's uncle! His cell was in his wife's name. How was I supposed to know that? I moved on to the Ancestry website; not sure what I was looking for there. I just didn't feel like I knew him. I did see the marriage certificate for him and his wife, but nothing else stood out. I wasn't sure what I was looking for but I wanted it to make sense somehow. I wanted to find an admission for psychiatric help! I wanted anything to take this feeling of being stupid away from me. After all that was said and done to me, he NEVER tried to reach out to explain or apologize.

One day after work I decided to do a drive by. I drove over to his apartment to see if he still lived there since I busted him that Sunday morning. According to Olivia, she had spoken to Deb who said they were moving. I pulled in; both Deb and Tony's trucks where there. I got sick on the stomach instantly, opened my door and let it out. I had no business coming here. What in the hell was I thinking, looking thirsty! I can't believe she would stay with someone like him. Deep down I wanted him to be sitting in there alone and miserable. I stopped acting like a fool, put my car in drive and headed to the house. As I was leaving the parking lot I saw Olivia turning in. She blew the horn and slowed down like she was going to stop. I threw my hand up and kept it moving. Not today!

Focus

I was trying to get my life back on track and focus on my work. I was doing ok while I was at work. I didn't think much of the situation since I had 23 employees to focus on. My support team was still fully active. I would get emails, text and calls daily to check on my mental status. Keesha would call also; she was feeling a type of way.

"I shouldn't have given him your number."

"I told you that you could. It's not your fault he was a sociopath."

"Girl, Kyle was even shocked shitless when I told him what happened."

All I keep telling myself is that I am glad that my girls were there with me when it all went down, because I don't think anyone would have believed me.

"I need to get back to work but thanks for calling to check on me" I said right after I told her what Ray had told me about the grandkids and other daughter that none of us knew about. I remember asking her to breathe; she was in utter shock.

She kept saying "Dee you are not serious? Girl you have got to be kidding."

I went back to doing my quality review on one of my team members when I received the text from Olivia to call her when I could. I looked at my phone wondering what the hell else she could possibly have to tell me. *I will* I placed my phone back on my desk as I shook my head in disbelief. I probably shouldn't have called her but I did. Curiosity killed the cat.

"Hey Olivia, can you talk now?"

"Yes, Dee I'm not trying to make you mad or dig up bad feelings. I needed to tell you what they are saying. I don't know if you still have your ring but you need sell it and anything else that can get him out of your spirit. Dee he is not right. I guess his tramp wanted to make peace with me. She was like" Hey can I talk to you? I don't know how you and Dee know each other but Tony gave her a friendship ring and she took it wrong." Dee, I almost slapped her. Hell I saw the pics on your page. I told her I saw the pics and she was like "She must have cropped them to look like that." She was saying that he is all hers now and that they are going to upgrade her ring since your little friendship ring looked too much like hers. While we were talking he came out the apartment and said that I could tell you anything now that he is free to be with Deb. "I don't know why Dee thought I would want to be with her, I don't date plump girls." Now she had my attention. I know damn well he did not call me plump! I am in a comfortable size 10, and with his big ass stomach?! Mother fuuuuuck! "I need to end this call quickly" I thought.

"Olivia, I don't think I want to know any more about what he is doing or with whom. I am trying to move forward in my life and forget these last 2 yrs ever happened. I know that conversation was uncomfortable for you, but I am so done with the whole thing. I have to sell the dress and the ring. I hope to recoup some of my money when I do and at this point I don't want to talk about him anymore. I have to go. Bye."
"Ok Dee, I just thought I would tell you."

"No problem; I'm just tired of it all. Have a great afternoon." I hung up and threw my phone in the passenger seat.
(UGHHHHHHHHHHHHHHHH!)

Reality

I had a hard time sleeping that night and the next couple of nights. I wasn't quite sure why I was restless. Maybe I needed to purge all items concerning him out of my "spirit" as Olivia said. I still had the gifts he'd given me, the wedding dress and the ring. I hadn't thought much about any of it since I still had them packed from my move. I decided that I would not get up at 3 am to do this but first thing in the morning it is on! Miraculously I drifted right back to sleep. I'm up early even though I haven't slept more than 5 solid hours. I grabbed my laptop and waited for it to power on. My first task was to list my wedding dress on Craigslist, Amazon and Ebay. I needed to get this out of my house. Next I gathered all of the stuffed animals, clothes, and Michael Kors bag, placed them in a garbage bag to take to Goodwill. I am going to take the ring to the jewelry store today for an appraisal. I jumped in the shower feeling a little better today than the past 3 days. I felt good about the decision to get those items out of "my spirit". I hoped to recoup some of the expense of the move. It will not replace the pain and betrayal but it will be a good start. My first stop was to Goodwill where I utilized the drive up, so I wouldn't have to worry about parking. Saturday mornings are crazy there. After the attendant insisted on me taking a receipt I was on my way to the mall to have the jewelry store appraise the ring. It was a gorgeous day, the sky was so blue and not a cloud in the sight. This is why I loved Charlotte; a November day and the high was supposed to be 60. I guess everybody wanted to get out and enjoy an early start because the lot was half way full at 11 am. I found a spot in front of Dick's Sporting, grabbed my things and walked into the mall. Northlake Mall was fairly new to this area and since I wasn't as familiar with it, I went to the directory board to see which jewelry store was closest to where I entered. Standing there I laughed to myself; my daughter would have been so embarrassed to see me looking at the directory for a store.

Kids! I located Kay Jewelry that was a little ways down the hall. I walked in and was thankful they were not crowded yet. A very nicely dressed male associate asked me if I needed help. "Yes; do you appraise jewelry on the weekend or do I need an appointment?"

"Yes ma'am we can do an appraisal today. My name is Paul."

"My name is Diane Simpson" I replied.

"May I see the ring?"

"Sure, here it is."

"I will be right back or you can come in the back with me."

"I'll look around; I may decide to put the center diamond in something else" I said.

"Great! If you need anything Alice will help you" he said as he pointed to another associate.

I started walking around the store looking into the cases of necklaces, earrings and bracelets. Nothing stood out much and by the time I looked into the 2nd case, Paul was back.

"Can I speak to you in the back?"

"Sure" I replied as I followed him toward the back with a sickening feeling in the pit of my stomach. Did his ass steal this shit? Oh hell no, I'm not going to jail for no damn body" I thought angrily!

"Ms. Simpson, I don't know how to tell you this."

"Tell me what?" I uttered as I snapped back.

"These diamonds are not real..."

"Wait…what?"
"No ma'am. As a matter of fact the entire ring is not white gold, or sterling silver...it's….it's nothing. It's just some type of plated metal."
"HAHAHA!!!" I begin laughing uncontrollably. Why I laughed like that I have absolutely no idea. I felt like the earth removed itself from underneath me and I was floating. This shit cannot be real!!!! "Paul, I don't care what you do with that thing; I don't want it. Thank you and I apologize for wasting your time." With that I turned around and marched out of there with my head held high. "This is some serious bullshit!"

By the time I got in my car the tears had started falling. I didn't know him; I just didn't! I beat my steering wheel up!!! I had to pull myself together so I could get back home safely. It seemed as though the tears would never stop and I cried until they ran dry. I checked my eyes in the visor mirror, pulled out my shades, and placed them on so that I could drove off. The guy who had pulled in the empty spot beside me must thought I had lost it. That's why when I saw him debating if he should come over and check on me I made it easy for him and pulled off. On my way home I prayed for understanding. The verse that my mom told me once she dropped me off at school came to mind; Proverbs 3:5-6 KJV "Trust in the Lord with all thine heart, and lean not to our own understanding. In all thy ways acknowledge him, and he shall direct thy paths." "God I need the understanding now. I don't know why or how I am going to be able to make it through this situation. God I feel like I am losing my footing every day. I have to be strong for the kids. Please take over this situation. AMEN."
When I got home I did a mass text to my girls and my sis, "The damn ring is fake!!! #thatisall I tossed my phone on the bed.

The next day was Saturday; my cleaning day.
"Hey kids turn on the music and let's clean this apartment like we use to clean the house."

"Ok mom," they sang together! Alicia Keys' "New Day" was playing and that was right on time!

"Turn it up! I yelled."
It is amazing what the power of true love can do. At that moment there was no sadness or memory of the storm we'd just endured. Peace had come back into our lives and I knew God was smiling on us. We cleaned that apartment, sung our songs, and danced until we were laughing and talking like we use to; before "The Day I Said Yes."

A Reading Group Guide

"THE DAY I SAID YES..."

1. What lesson/lessons did you gain from this read?

2. At the end of the day are women really willing to "put up" with the shenanigans of men, or do women take heart over common sense?

3. Looking back over the story, what early signs did you pick up on? Which ones were clearly being justified or ignored by Diane?

4. What would you say was the lowest thing Diane found out that Tony did?

5. What would you do if you found out that your fiancé approached your kids to ask for your hand in marriage knowing that all that he had presented was a lie?

6. Tony presented himself as being the same old Tony that Diane knew as a teen when they talked. Even after she asked the probing questions his answers sounded normal. Is it possible for someone of that age to be the "same" person they were over 20 years ago?

7. Which character do you feel is more at fault; Tony or Diane?

8. We all remember our "first love". As an adult and knowing what you know now, was it love, lust or a mixture of both?

Made in the USA
Charleston, SC
04 November 2014